Canoeing
the
Mountain

Canoeing
the
Mountain

Gifts from the Waters

Phil Weir

Wildwaters Publishing

WILDWATERS

Published in Canada by : Wildwaters Publishing
106 – 55 Blackberry Drive, New Westminster, BC
www.wildwaterspublishing.com
Printed in the United States of America

Front cover artwork image by Dan Weir (after photo by Pat O'Shea)
Cover design by Phil Weir and by Jim Bisakowski: BookDesign.ca
Text design and typesetting by Jim Bisakowski: BookDesign.ca
Back cover photo by Pat O'Shea
Group photo by unknown photographer from rafter-kayaker group
Author photo by Phil Weir

Library and Archives Canada Cataloguing in Publication
Weir, Phil, 1951-, author
        Canoeing the Mountain : gifts from the waters / Phil Weir.

Issued in print and electronic formats.
ISBN 978-0-9920665-0-5 (pbk.).--ISBN 978-0-9920665-1-2 (mobi).--
ISBN 978-0-9920665-2-9 (epub)

        1. Canoes and canoeing--Northwest Territories--Mountain River.
2. Whitewater canoeing--Northwest Territories--Mountain River. I. Title.

GV776.15.N57W45 2014   797.12209719'3   C2013-905848-6
                                                      C2013-905849-4

Before starting:

This book should not be used as a guidebook or a trip planner. Don't rely on these words or your own luck to see you through. Luck can change quicker than the weather. Distances and other information may not be accurate, and due to many factors, it truly is the case that the Mountain River is a different river every day. For any adventure in the wild, a traveller should first do their own pre-trip homework, gain the needed skills, collect up-to-date information, including input and risk assessment from professional guides, and plan carefully. Once on-site, they should scout whenever possible, make their own observations, weigh all the circumstances and adapt. Even so, there will surely be surprises. Stay positive.

To Jill,

Jody, Daniel and Patrick

Let's go paddling.

This might best be told in the woods somewhere, in the evening, round a campfire. The tents would be ready, but we wouldn't be sleepy yet. After eating we'd sit and tell our stories. Some tales are so long in the telling that a single evening's campfire isn't enough, so I've written this one down. Take a seat by the fire for a while. Smell the woodsmoke. Listen to the water lapping nearby. Come along.

This story is true
From my point of view
As true as memories can be.
Through much time and space
Good fortune and grace
These things remain
Part of me.

It could have been this year, or any year really. There's a kind of timeless thing about canoe trips. But our Mountain River trip in Canada's Northwest Territories was in 1991. I was 40. More than two decades later I'm happy to say that this beautiful wilderness river continues to run wild and free for its entire length, the same as it did during our trip. The Mountain River can still be paddled, with caution and respect, from source to mouth.

Phil Weir

PROLOGUE

The greatest gift was the well.

It started to be part of me long before I went on the trip, even before we started planning. Some sort of a dream of it had been passed along by movies, books, stories and pictures; by other travelers who had tasted the wilderness and felt the need to share their experience of something so wonderful and profound it can hardly be described. On our journey, what I came to call "the well" became deeper and richer for me. Since then it has grown deeper still. I can fly to it in my mind at any time. In the accurate phrasing of Indigenous traditions: "It is good medicine," medicine that I can scarcely understand, but which is beautiful and powerful. Sometimes I feel it in obvious ways; most times it is subtle, almost forgotten, but it forms part of who I am. For this I am deeply thankful. I have drunk the healing potion of the wild, and will never be the same.

W e were eight friends, listed here by canoe, stern first, in the order in which we usually paddled:

Otto Schreiber,	Kevin Conway
Phil Weir,	Roger Michon
Bert Waslander,	Odile Waslander
Pat O'Shea,	Brian Conway

After a year of preparation, our group flew northwest from Ottawa to Edmonton, then north to Yellowknife, and from there further northwest to tiny Norman Wells on the Mackenzie River. We travelled the last leg, to the start of our canoeing, using small float planes which landed on tiny Willow Handle Lake, a primary source lake of the Mountain River, near the top of the Mackenzie Mountains. From there we were 18 amazing days on the water, canoeing a total of 302 kilometres, while descending 1140 metres to the mouth of the Mountain River at the Mackenzie. That descent of more than a vertical kilometre gave us almost continuous fast-flowing current, five-star whitewater, extreme challenges, and a fabulous ride.

We paddled in pairs, using four open 16 foot canoes rented from an outfitter in Norman Wells. The rest of our gear and food we brought north ourselves. Two of us slept in each of our four tents. Three of these were four-person, and Odile and Bert, who were husband and wife, shared a two-person. The roominess of having four tents gave us back-up: if a tent got damaged or lost, we would be able to modify and sleep three to a tent. Like all of our many precautions, we hoped this wouldn't be put to the test.

Our ages ranged from early thirties to early fifties. Everyone was fit and had several years of camping and paddling experience, plus whitewater canoeing training, and certifications. Five also had First Aid qualifications. In meetings during the lead-up year we had covered a broad range of topics, such as equipment, transportation, menus, maps, and emergency wilderness First Aid. The group also did a practice trip together on the Madawaska River near Ottawa in the early spring before our trip. As we left for the Northwest Territories, we believed we were well prepared, in the ways that a group should be for this kind of remote trip. We understood the risks clearly: if we got into trouble there would be no outside help. Our preparations, individual strengths, and the group's ability to adapt would be all we would have to see us through; that, and the good grace of the river.

Otto, Pat, Odile and I were all high school teachers. Roger and Kevin worked for the same school board in media production. Odile's husband Bert was a federal civil servant, and Brian, who was Kevin's brother, worked for CP Rail (Canadian Pacific) in computer operations.

Otto was our most experienced paddler, and the trip leader. Ten years older than myself, he had initiated me into whitewater canoeing a few years before this trip. I started as a teacher-supervisor on outings with his high school Outdoor Education Club, and later became a co-teacher of his ground-breaking Outdoor Education high school credit course. Otto taught everyone well, usually with good-hearted humour. Though he could sometimes be gruff like a bear, he was usually gentle as a teddy, and had an air of leadership. He also had a long history of helping "rough diamonds," sometimes called "challenging youth," to experience success in the Ottawa school system, including in the Outdoor Classroom. Maybe this was part of the reason he invited me along on his Mountain River trip. I was still a bit of a whitewater rough diamond myself at the time, relatively new to the sport, but keen and learning fast. I'm glad he gave me the chance. I've tried to remember this, and frequently invite others to come along on my trips.

Pat, or as we often called him, Paddy, was also a high school teacher, and had canoe-tripped with Otto quite a bit. The year before our Mountain River trip they had paddled the Nahanni River together with friends. Pat had also taught Outdoor Education clubs over the years. He had a wry sense of humour, frequently the "groaner" variety, but it was always delivered with a twinkle in his Irish eyes.

Bert and Odile had decades of living and tripping together under their paddles. Odile, the only woman on the trip, put up with seven woodsy guys very well. A common practice on long canoe trips is to split couples, and have them paddle in different boats, but Odile and Bert did fine together throughout our trip. Bert was also known to come out with a few puns, which made some of us wonder if he was perhaps distantly related to Paddy. Odile's cheerful, steady, optimistic personality was a constant inspiration and boost to the whole group, especially during stressful times.

The two brothers Kevin and Brian had whitewater experience before the trip, but not as much as Otto, Pat, Bert or Odile. Kevin paddled out in front of everyone in the bow of Otto's lead canoe. Brian paddled in the bow of Pat's canoe, which was our last, or sweep boat. Both put out steady power, made sudden steering decisions when needed, and reliably helped out their stern paddlers. Kevin's quiet-spoken, calm manner, even when under pressure, and his kindness and tolerance, were especially appreciated by me, since I was fortunate to have him as my tent partner. Brian, with his burly moustache and beard, in some ways resembled the cartoon character Yosemite Sam, but he didn't pack pistols or have a hair-trigger temper. He usually preferred fishing, a quiet smoke, or a good chuckle to stressing or worrying.

My own canoe partner Roger also had whitewater experience before our Mountain River trip. He and Kevin had helped Otto make some great educational videos about Outdoor Education and safe whitewater trips with groups of high school students. Roger is as tough and dependable as they come. I couldn't have asked for a better partner. Witty and quick thinking, he's a determined bulldog when it comes to sticking at a difficult task and, "gettin' 'er done." You can count on him, always, and I certainly did. The conversations, banter and camaraderie were unforgettable fun, as our paddling learning curves went sky-high together on that fabulous river. Most meaningful to me, when I made my mistakes – and yes, there were a few – my buddy Roger forgave me. What more can a friend hope for?

I suppose I had a fair background in whitewater canoeing, camping, First Aid and teaching Outdoor Ed. when we started out on our Mountain River trip – but I had a lot to learn.

———•—•———

I

There were gifts I could touch with my hands, visions, scents, sounds and silences; lasting gifts to my heart and to my spirit; increased depths of knowing, of understanding, and of feeling.

———•—•———

I still believe Roger and I were the luckiest ones. We got to be the advance scouts, the first to fly from Norman Wells up into the mountains, riding in a little single-prop Pilatus Porter plane that we dubbed "the Platypus," while the other six had to keep waiting on the dock for their larger Twin Otter. It had been borrowed by Northwest Territories forest fire management authorities, but wasn't back yet when our little Platypus came buzzing in.

After the long previous day and night, spent hopping from plane, to airport, and back to yet another plane, our group had camped a few hours beside the float plane base. It had taken us 16 hours to get there from Ottawa. After landing at the small Norman Wells airport at midnight, and schlepping our big load of gear by pickup truck taxis to the nearby base, we set up our four tents for the first time in the wee hours of the morning, and all crashed for a short nap. Only four hours later we got up, wolfed down a quick breakfast, broke camp, and prepared everything for our fly-in to the headwaters.

It was the day we had dreamed about for a long time. Anticipation, sleep-loss, jet lag, and the wonderful clean northern air, had everyone in great spirits. Although this was the start of our second day since leaving home, we called it "Day 1," because it would be the first of our paddling days, our actual canoe trip.

Unfortunately, after the morning rush to get everything to the dock on time, we learned that both of our planes were delayed, having been sequestered for fire-fighting work. There was no predicted arrival time. We slowed right down and shifted into waiting mode. It gradually sank in that this was going to be a long delay. Fire work is unpredictable, and obviously a much higher priority than a group of recreational canoeists. We left our gear at the base and went off to tour the town.

Norman Wells is built on the eastern shore of the huge Mackenzie River. It lies just a few kilometres north of the 65th parallel, and is roughly 450 kilometres south of Inuvik, the Beaufort Sea, and the Arctic Ocean. As a plane flies, it is 375 km north of the Nahanni River, 680 km northwest of Yellowknife, and 1520 km north of Edmonton. There is no direct flight to Norman Wells from Ottawa, but if there was, the straight-line distance would be 3760 kilometres.

We learned that the "Wells" that gave the town its name are oil drilling wells, located on man-made islands in the middle of the Mackenzie. These are in full operation and draw oil directly up from deep below the river bed. Besides this core industry, the town also serves as a regional hub for tourism, government facilities, supplies and services.

Our first group photographs were taken out in front of the wonderful little Norman Wells Museum. These classic "before" pictures show all eight of us wearing fresh, clean trip clothes. Every face beams with excitement and anticipation. The stage was fully set.

After a few hours of touring we got restless, and headed back to the float plane dock to wait. Everyone wanted to get busy doing what we had come all this way to do, to get up in those beautiful high mountains we could see rising abruptly just across on the far side of the Mackenzie. We wanted to be canoeing the Mountain River.

I jumped up when I heard the low pitched hum in the distance. Roger leapt up beside me. It was the little Platypus returning to the base, seven hours late. Hardly able to contain our excitement, we watched it come closer, then land with a fan of spray just offshore. The motor revved loudly for a moment, then wound down as it slowly pulled alongside the dock. Our ride had arrived!

The pilot and staff at the base did a fast turn-around, and in half an hour it was fully prepped, ready to go on. Our canoe was roped securely to one of the pontoon legs, and our packs and some of the group gear stuffed into the small cabin. Roger and I said quick goodbyes to the others and hopped in.

We grinned ear-to-ear out the windows as the plane taxied slowly down the lake. Then the pilot turned us around, and with a roar, accelerated past the base. Waving like delighted kids in a big yellow school bus, we zoomed past our friends left waiting on the dock. Rising from the spray, the plane banked sharply to the left, westward. We were on our way.

The noisy hot-rod buzzed and bounced, sometimes bucking like a bronco as it lifted towards the top of the Backbone Range of the Mackenzie Mountains. We were bound for the very edge of the Continental Divide, which also forms the border between the Northwest Territories and the Yukon. All moving water on this side of these mountains would flow eventually to the east, and north to the Arctic Ocean, while just over their summits everything would flow westward, towards the Pacific. Very near this alpine watershed divide, we would land on pristine Willow Handle Lake.

In less than a minute after take-off, Norman Wells and its surrounding buildings had dropped away and disappeared behind. The huge Mackenzie River and its wide flood plain quickly did the same. From then on we could see no signs of human beings, or their activities, in any direction: no roads, vehicles, buildings, machines, mines – no traces.

I had never before been anywhere where there was such a vast absence of the effects of people. Flying lower than a double engine plane, and much lower than any jet, we barely scooped over the many ridges and peaks. We gazed with wonder and excitement. The wilderness, with all its splendour, grandeur, and details, was right there, only a short distance away, right outside our windows. Except for the noisy bug in which we were travelling, we were totally in the wild. Surrounding us in every direction was unspoiled nature: Mother Earth. We stared down over wave after wave of summits and mountain spines, washed with cloud shadows of grey, light brown, and forest green. Near the highest peaks, the rocks looked slate blue, and deep down in the bottoms of some of the valleys, we saw glinting back at us, the bright silver, multi-braided threads of rivers.

Along with awe and joy, I was flooded with an unfamiliar sensation that surprised me: it felt like I was coming home. This tingling feeling reminded me how much I love being in nature, in natural spaces. It is such a core part of who I am. Even when in the middle of a big city, it's still so important just to know places like this exist out there somewhere. To spend time in the wild is always restorative to my spirit, like having a long drink of lovely cold water when very thirsty. As I flew along on our spectacular 90-minute ride, I savoured my inner spirit being filled to overflowing from nature's immense well.

Roger and I stared out the windows, laughing and snapping pictures, giving each other high-fives and thumbs-up. Diving in and out of white puffy clouds, we passed through alternating spells of rain and sunshine, heading for the source, the beginning of the watershed. In what seemed like a short time, the pilot pointed downwards with his thumb, eased off on the throttle, and started to descend. Shining below, we saw a tiny mirror of light. Dropping out of the sky like a big mechanical goose, the plane flew into the middle of the bottom of a huge natural bowl, within a giant circle of high mountain peaks. With a splash and hiss, our floats gently touched the waters of Willow Handle Lake.

In the golden, bright, northern summer afternoon light of 8:00 pm, our engine revved loudly, then dropped off almost to silence. We taxied slowly towards a low, rough, wooden dock located beside a level area that had apparently been used as a hunt camp sometime in the recent past. This was the only spot on the little lake with any visible signs of previous human activity. We jumped out and the three of us unloaded everything in ten minutes.

As soon as all of our gear was on shore, including our canoe and paddles, the pilot and plane left us. The Platypus taxied noisily back down the lake, picked up speed, and gracefully lifted into the air. Quickly becoming small against the sky, it banked sharply to the right, rose a little higher, and disappeared behind a mountain. Moments later the buzz of its motor faded to nothing.

Roger and I were suddenly alone. We stood silently in the stillness, two small travellers within the huge, all-encompassing natural environment. More joy and gratitude filled me with every breath of that fresh, spruce-scented air. Those first mountain breaths – I still remember, can still smell, still feel inside my lungs. I expect I always will. It was the evening of July 10, Day 1. For almost three weeks there would be no going back.

This kind of feeling can't be bought. You have to work for it. Our slow 360° visual pans took in outstanding beauty everywhere, at every elevation. There was no road or trail that we could see: nothing around the lake, nor leading through the bushes. On our topographic map the summits of this ring of multi-coloured mountains surrounding the lake were shown to be 2000 metres above sea level. From the water's surface, the mountains started rising at 1100 metres. So, as we scanned from lake to mountain tops, we were looking upwards 900 metres, almost a vertical kilometre. But numbers were irrelevant during these moments. Roger and I had known it was going to be good, but this was vastly better than expected. Every view displayed a stunning postcard image of the wild. And there we were: the only people.

Low plants and shrubs ringed the lake. A little further back stood a few short, spindly black spruce trees that seemed to be trying, but failing, to march up the mountainsides from the sheltered valley. These got shorter as they climbed, first shrinking to low bushes, then completely disappearing at the tree line. This distinctly visible transition line was only 100 metres above the elevation where we stood. There, all green stopped, leaving only bare rock, in a beautiful palette of colours, all the way to the summits. Perhaps a few lichens might live at those higher elevations, and there might be the occasional low alpine flower, but that would be all. Just over the peaks on the western rim of the bowl lay the Yukon, and the beginning of drainage towards the West Coast.

With the airplane noise gone, replacing it was deep silence. Like a long pause in a symphony, I found myself waiting for the next loud chord, but none came. The only sounds were the occasional faint chirps of small birds. Now and then there was a little flutter of their wings in the waterside bushes. The ringing in my ears began to fade, as my hearing gradually started to readjust to the natural world. The word "peace" came into my mind.

Emotionally I felt as if I was being wrapped in a soft, treasured blanket, a special, almost forgotten blanket from long ago, yet so familiar. As I had felt on the plane, I again experienced the warm tingling sensation of coming home, to a home I'd been away from for a very long time. I felt welcomed.

This was one of those times of strong emotions when a traveller knows they are extremely fortunate. It's a feeling of true richness. We had made it. We were at the put-in. All of our individual and group preparations had been done. Our gear, food and canoe were ready. Friends were on the way. We were set to live and travel outdoors in the summertime, in the Northwest Territories, for almost three weeks. In front of us lay the whole Mountain River and its watershed.

I burned a little sweetgrass, which I always do with respect. Since learning about it from Algonquin and Mohawk friends several years ago, I've always carried a braid of sweetgrass and a lighter with me in a plastic bag on canoe trips. Usually I carry it in my pants pocket or life jacket (PFD) pocket. Often I'll burn some at the put-in, beside the water's edge, or at significant places or times along the way. I've often joked with my high school students that it is perfectly legal to burn sweetgrass, which smells lovely and sweet. It has been respectfully burned in North America for at least ten thousand years. I try to keep that respect going, and am thankful to have been told a few things about this special medicine.

As the smoke drifted gently from the end of the braid I thought of many people who would love to be there with me. I felt so lucky. I also thought of the generations of people who had come before us to this place, and of the people who would come after us, in the future. I thought of how this amazing wilderness would still be here long after our group was gone. Thank goodness.

An important teaching that I've learned from elders is: when you smell the smoke of sweetgrass, when it drifts over you, it is a purification. It clears the head and the heart, and helps us to think and speak our inner truth. It reminds us of other good times, and of the fact that everything, like the braid, is interconnected. Most especially, it reminds us that, "Everything will be alright, but not necessarily how we think." Burning sweetgrass is a sign of deep respect: respect for oneself, for each other, for Mother Earth, for history, for the lakes, rivers, oceans, all water, all land, fire, earth, sky, the forests, for all the birds and animals: respect for everything. It's right that we show our respect – especially when in special places, and at special times.

I felt humbled and privileged to be able to stand there and burn sweetgrass in this place, and inwardly said, "Meegwetch." In simplest terms this very ancient Native American word, which has several spelling variations, means, "Thank you", or "I thank you." There are so many ways to feel thankful. I believe that, regardless of one's particular beliefs or the vocabulary used, it's always best to somehow recognize when we have received gifts, luck, special compensation, blessings, an alignment of the stars, or whatever other label we choose to call our good fortunes. It is also worthwhile to sometimes simply pay our respect without any implications of a present, past, or future reward. After the braid had smouldered quietly in my hand for a few minutes, with its fragrant, gentle smoke drifting and swirling around me, I let it burn out and cool down, and packed it away in my pocket.

Walking slowly away from the water's edge, Roger and I began hauling the gear to the spot where we would set up the group camp. But this energetic spurt only lasted for a single load, about three minutes, because we both stopped spontaneously and stared all around us again. We stood quietly, calmly, looking, smelling, listening, and feeling.

It had rained recently. In the clean, still air I noticed that I could hear myself slowly inhaling and exhaling. Then I realized with surprise that I could also hear my heart beating. The human-centred, motor-centred, world was continuing to fade.

Knowing the others would soon fly in, we savoured our time of solitude in this heaven. It would've been a delight to camp there on our own for a day or two, or even a month. In the window of soft gold sunlight before the next coming shower, we quietly wandered the green shore of the source lake for a few minutes longer, having our private thoughts.

Twenty minutes after our plane left, clouds and a light mist rolled in, spurring us into action again. The gear was quickly organized, and we pitched the large blue and white, waterproof nylon group tarp. Then at 9:00 p.m., only an hour after Roger and I had arrived, we heard their plane coming in the distance. A couple of minutes later, the big Twin Otter splashed down, carrying our six friends, plus their three canoes and all the rest of the gear. We welcomed our smiling comrades with handshakes and hugs, and helped unload.

Their flight in the larger twin engine plane had taken less than an hour compared to our ninety minute ride. Flying a little higher, and with fewer bumps and turns, they had flown right up part of the Mountain River valley, without needing to zigzag and barely skim over peaks and ridges as our plane had done. Roger and I quietly agreed that it didn't sound like as much fun as our bronco ride.

With all of us together again, camp quickly became louder, busier, more festive. Solo canoe trips and group trips are each good in their own ways. Now the dynamics of the larger group experience transformed what had been our near-solo time. It was great to be with friends again, ready to go, and also to witness their first wide-eyed appreciation of the beauty of this glorious place. Everyone was in fabulous spirits. Otto put in a line, and in only ten minutes caught two fish: graylings, each about a foot long.

After setting up, and eating a quick dinner, I slipped our canoe into the water and went out alone onto the lake for my first paddle of the trip. It was magical: a quiet, deeply moving, evening solo on the smooth, glass surface. I could feel inside that this entire sensory and emotional experience was being recorded, engraved into my life-time memory bank.

Drifting slowly, I soaked everything in: the strong connection between the water, earth, sky, and myself. It may sound corny, but it was about the oneness of it all. The light mist in the spruce air gave a soft, almost mystical haziness to everything. To me, the words "spiritual" and "divine" conjure up moments like this. I felt exceptionally blessed to have the opportunity to be there, for my short time, in the centre of that great mountain bowl, in the middle of that pure source lake, in my canoe, alone, safe, calm, drifting, at peace. The mist moistened my face from the sky above; the water and the earth held me up from below.

I had an urge to share this wonderful experience with the others, and briefly thought of rushing back to camp and encouraging them to hop in their boats for a paddle too. But the peace of the moment prevailed. I realized that the best thing I could do with this time was to fully appreciate it myself.

Eventually tiredness began to displace wonder. In the glow of early twilight I looked at my watch and saw with surprise that it was 11:00 p.m.! There was no need for a flashlight as I crawled into the tent for the night. Kevin was already sleeping.

I closed my eyes just after midnight, dreaming of adventures to come, and remembering the wonderful tingling feeling I had experienced on the plane, and again when standing on the shore: nature's blanket, wrapping softly around, welcoming me home.

2

I was given a deeper appreciation of the fact that every moment, of every day, is a gift. When surrounded by beauty on a lovely morning this is undeniable. But when the weather has socked in for days, and the body aches, and fears of what's to come surround, it is still undeniable: every moment, of every day, is a gift.

We would pick up stones by the riverside, marveling at all the colours, how they had been rounded, how the sun glints off them, how every single one is different. Coming from somewhere else and left there by the water, can they be seen as gifts? Can something be a gift if it is not left intentionally for someone by some entity, some being, or mystical force?

Acceptance came over me eventually. "Don't even ask," is the answer. Just feel gratitude. Accept and appreciate. Know that you are blessed: by being alive, by being wherever you are, by whatever has come to your hands, eyes or heart.

———•◦•———

Next morning we all started slowly. Altitude adjustments, jet lag and fatigue had kicked in, and most slept late. But what a fabulous first morning in the mountains it was! The air was again deliciously clean and fresh as I crawled out in the early, misty twilight, hoping to have a few more moments of solitude. A light rain had recently ended. The rest of camp was still asleep. Wandering quietly by the lake I felt myself glow inside as I looked at a marvelous vision by the water's edge: our four canoes lay there, upside-down, nestled together, waiting.

In the still air, there was again only the occasional flitting of little wings. What a beautiful place these birds have to live! I thought of how they would still be living here after we had moved on. Soon there were a few more sounds: a tent zipper opening and closing, the crack of a firewood branch, the bump of a pot, a few low words of conversation.

Thin wisps of white cloud swirled gently above the lake's smooth surface. These gradually lifted, dissipating, until within half an hour the sky had cleared to bright blue. It was as if immense curtains were opening on this vast wilderness stage. Eventually sunlight spot-lit the mountain tops in brilliant colours of gold, brown, silver and grey, then worked its way down the mountainsides to touch the lake.

I'm not much of fisherman, but thinking of my nine year old son Daniel who loves fishing, I tossed my line in, and dreamed of maybe coming back some day with him, or even with our whole family. I caught a grayling in less than ten minutes, and ate it with my breakfast. Delicious! As it turned out, this was the only fishing I did on the trip.

After breakfast we prepared the canoes, gradually packed up, and hauled everything to the water's edge. We carefully loaded our packs, equipment and big plastic food barrels into the black rental boats. There were smiles all around when we saw that everything fit.

Before leaving, we walked over the camping area and carefully "no traced the place." This process includes picking up, and either packing out or burning, every single bit of human garbage: every bread-bag tie, wrapper, bottle cap, bit of plastic, and cigarette butt. Although it takes some getting used to at first, the process of "no tracing" sometimes includes packing out other people's garbage as well. If we don't do it who will? It's a form of stewardship, an acceptance of personal responsibility to care for the wild. Plus it leaves a person feeling good. At this particular campsite there weren't very many things for us to pick up, but we found a few. We packed them out with us, and left the place cleaner than when we arrived.

It had been a lovely lazy morning but now everyone was keen to paddle. We got into our canoes at 2:00, and with smiles and anticipation, pushed off in bright sunshine onto the pure, calm waters of Willow Handle Lake. I love this time, just after launching, when the ready boat that I am in first floats off, beginning a day's paddle, or a longer trip. As motion begins, the bow, stern, and paddles each create little ripples and small twirling eddies. It is also a personal habit of mine at that time to turn my head, and glance back for a moment or two, taking a last quiet look, and remembering the places gone by. Then I paddle on.

A photograph of our group as we started out would be a great cover for some glossy magazine. Most of our clothing was spanking new, bought for the trip. The sun and warmth had caused many of us to leave our cold weather gear stowed in our packs for now, opting to wear t-shirts under our PFDs. Sunscreen had been liberally applied.

I wore a striped yellow and black bumble-bee t-shirt, keeping my new coral (pink) waterproof paddling jacket for later. In case things turned suddenly cold or wet, I wore red quick-dry polypropylene long john bottoms, which I called my "polyprop," under my grey nylon pants. Over the outside of my pant legs went blue neoprene knee pads. Keeping my feet warm, even if they got wet, were blue neoprene bootie socks, and my light blue, slip-on paddling shoes. This whole eclectic fashion statement was completed by a purple and white good-luck neck bandana, and my, fairly new, white, broad-rimmed canvas Tilly hat.

Gunslinger style, I wore a red throwbag around my waist, resting horizontally on the back of my hips. Stuffed with 60 feet of bright yellow floatable rope that plays out smoothly if the bag gets tossed, a throwbag looks like a small lower back pillow when not being used to rescue a person or a boat, or to make a clothesline, or maybe hold up a tarp. An oval metal carabiner clip or "biner" (pronounced "beener") was tied to the end of the rope that stuck out of the sack, ready to clip to something in a hurry. Two more biners hung from the cinch straps on either side of my PFD, for quick access.

I paddled in my usual position: which is on my knees, with my bum braced against the stern seat. Many people only use this "tripod" or "two-knees-and-a-bum" position if they are in rapids, wind or waves. But I've grown used to sitting this way. Of course my kneepads help. I find it safer to be down low, and also get more power in my strokes. You'll usually only see me sitting in the relaxed position that I call the "happy fisherman," with my bum on the seat and knees up wide apart in front of me, if I am taking a break in calm water. Some paddlers' avoid the tripod position whenever possible, because their knees or ankles get painfully cramped. I sympathize with the very real pain they feel. But if approaching whitewater, or if their canoe is out in the wind or waves, a good paddler will always drop down into the much safer tripod position, making the boat's centre of gravity lower. On this calm day, either position would have been fine. But I like canoeing this way. For me it's like wearing my PFD: I just do it all the time.

Inside our canoe my full one-litre plastic water bottle was clipped to a small rope loop on the stern thwart right in front of me. On the bottom sat my small green canvas army surplus day bag, binered in by its strap. It held a few sealed zip-locked plastic bags containing my prized SLR camera, my small personal journal, toilet paper, a spare lighter, a box of waterproof matches, and a few other small items.

Of course the others looked dashing too. We all had beautiful brand new, wide-bladed whitewater paddles made out of laminated wood, with slightly curved wooden T-handgrips, and hard urethane blade tips. These had been kindly donated to our group by Grey Owl Paddles. For now, I and a few others used our spare aluminum-shafted, tough plastic-bladed "Mohawk" paddles. Each person wore their own throwbag, in various designer colours. Along with the paddles that were being used, and two other spares stowed, each boat also carried a couple of bailer buckets made from re-used plastic windshield washer antifreeze containers. With their caps still on tight and bottoms cut off, they made great water scoopers, and were kept handy, clipped into the front and back of each boat on short ropes. Lastly, tied to the tips of each bow and stern, were painters: six-metre lengths of yellow floatable rope, coiled loosely, ready to grab.

Besides the paddlers, each boat carried their two big canoe packs, a tent, a large, heavy food barrel, or the equivalent in group gear, plus a day pack and water bottle for each person. Everything had been made as waterproof, or "bombproof," as possible, using store-bought heavy duty dry-bags, or double-bagged plastic bag liners. Once river-tripping, all of our gear would be clipped in, using biners through straps, handles or harnesses. These biners were then clipped to a tether rope, which, in a capsized situation, would either keep the gear with the boat, or could be quickly released to free everything. Theoretically all packs, gear and food were prepared to withstand being fully immersed, without any of the contents getting wet. Because there was always some air in the packs, in the event of an upset, they should all stay afloat, tethered to the boat, until untied or cut free.

Our large, thick, blue plastic food and equipment barrels sported heavy duty back-pack-style harnesses and strong plastic handles. They were specially made for this kind of back-country canoe-tripping by Trailhead, an outfitter store in Ottawa. With their tough construction, rubber seal gaskets, and thick black lids which close tight using lockable metal clamps, these barrels are waterproof. They are also generally considered bear-proof. These wonderful inventions carry large heavy loads, and when used with care, common sense and cleanliness, they eliminate the need to hang food when camping.

It only took us fifteen minutes to paddle the short distance to the north end of the lake: barely a warm-up. We stepped out onto the spongy, thick shore moss and bushes, and looked around for the portage trail that we had been told would lead us to a trickling headwaters stream with enough water to float our boats. Finding this was a little trickier than anticipated. There were several animal paths through the low bushes and tall grass, but these were the only trails we could see. We did our best, but ended up hiking around for probably about half a kilometre more than was needed. Some of this time was spent with boats on our heads, before we all got on the right track, so to speak.

Though confusing, the scene was beautiful. It was so rare to be in a place where there were no obvious human trails. Once again the heady smell of the evergreens filled the air. Because of the thick, low bushes some of the group wore "bear bells" around their necks or dangling from packs, to let any possible nearby furry inhabitants know that we were around, and hopefully scare them off. We saw none that day, but enjoyed the tinkling.

That walk to the beginning of the floatable water flow was to be the only portage of our entire 18-day trip, a real treat for 302 kilometres of river travel by canoe! Once we had gotten our bearings it only took three twenty minute trips to haul everything to the edge of the little creek.

Those of us who carried canoes on our heads couldn't help noticing that these black rentals were heavy beasts. The plastic Coleman tripping canoes appeared to be rugged whitewater boats, but they were a little unusual. Unlike the tough plastic ABS "foam sandwich" boats that we all paddled back home, these hulls were made out of a single sheet of thick, roto-molded plastic. The canoes also had lots of aluminum parts, including the gunwales, thwarts, and support posts that were under each thwart. The two flat seats were also made of aluminum, with a thin plastic pad on top. The support posts, not usually seen in a canoe, were also attached to a long skinny aluminum brace which ran along the centre of the entire floor of each boat. It seemed like all this aluminum was overdoing the reinforcement a bit, and it added weight. But we accepted that these were the boats we'd been given, and just hoped they would do the job ahead.

Our set of topographical maps was annotated with information that some experienced professional river-guide friends had given us, but no-one in our group had actually paddled this river before. This gave us the challenge and the pleasure of sorting several things out for ourselves. Finding the portage to the headwaters of moving navigable water was our group's first problem-solving exercise, and it went well. If someone were watching from above we would have looked like a small pod of black whale-backs, perhaps orcas, heaving, diving, and ploughing over the green sea of grass and bushes.

The narrow, shallow, crystal clear moving water that we eventually stood beside, with our line of loaded canoes, is called "Push-Pull Creek." Barely wider than a canoe at this point, we knew that this was it: the start of our 302 kilometre downriver run through the mountains. Everyone topped up their water bottles with the pure, cold water, and we toasted each other and the trip: "To the Mountain River!" So delicious! We drank our fill, and climbed into the canoes.

Otto and Kevin pushed off first and began floating with the gentle current. Roger and I waited a minute for them to get a few boat-lengths ahead, then let the water take our boat as well. Just behind, Bert and Odile also launched and followed, and lastly came Paddy and Brian. Like a wavy strung out line of ducks, we swirled around the narrow bends.

For the first ten minutes this was the tiniest, most shallow waterway I had ever floated a canoe on, not even deep enough for us to be able to properly use our paddles, so we mainly drifted. To steer, we would grab overhanging branches of bordering shrubs, or use our paddle blades to push off the pebbles on the bottom.

The creek soon widened to triple a canoe-width, and also began picking up speed. There was now enough volume to use a few shallow steering strokes without grounding out as we whipped down and around several blind turns lined with shrubs or tall grasses. True to the creek's name we had to jump out into ankle deep water several times to push and pull our canoe off the bottom. The water was so beautifully clear that it was invisible, and could only be seen when splashed or moved by a paddle.

Roger and I called back and forth to each other, and spent most of that first section laughing. Occasionally the bushes and other plant life that lined the stream were broken by small gravel beaches of round, shining, multi-coloured pebbles. When there were grassy openings we saw fantastic views of the colossal surrounding mountains.

Often Otto and Kevin's lead boat, or the canoes behind us, went out of sight for a few moments around a bend. During times without visual contact, we would listen carefully for any whistle signals as we paddled. When a boat came back into view we watched for any paddle signals. As water from other little creeks joined us along the way, Push-Pull continued to widen. We picked up speed, sailing around bend after bend in the brilliant sunshine.

After half an hour, Push-Pull flowed into a bigger tribu-tary of the Mountain River, called Black Feather Creek, and their combined flow became deeper, wider and stronger. This confluence was shown on our topographic maps simply as an intersection of thin lines. Neither was named, being too small.

Now and then we would all pull over, re-group, and chat. Sometimes we did this by "eddying-out" using the shore eddy, and beaching our canoes. The current by the side of a river is usually slower than the main current, and sometimes even runs in reverse. The difference between this slower backwards flow and the main downstream current, is often called a shore eddy, or a reverse current effect. Eddying-out using the shore eddy is a common moving-water manoeuvre, where a boat does a fast, whip-like, almost 180° turn, quite close to the river's edge. It is intended to get the boat out of the current in a hurry, and stop its downstream motion. In the last part of the turn the bow is nudged to shore, and the person in front hops onto dry land or into the shallows, while holding the bow line or bow grip. He or she then pulls the front of the canoe up onto the land just a little, but not much, because that makes it tippy. The bow-person holds the boat steady while the stern paddler climbs out, usually accomplished by crawling along the top of the gear on hands and knees. The entire turn and exit is done as a continuous motion, and allows a moving canoe to stop quickly at the side of a fast flowing river.

A couple of kilometres further along, Black Feather Creek was bordered on both sides by an icefield. Viewed from far away as a brilliant white object, we soon saw close up that it was made of compacted, bluish-white snow that was three metres deep in some parts. This beautiful glacier-like remnant of last winter continued on for a few hundred metres. Near its highest section, our little fleet pulled over on river-left, which is the left side of a river when going down a river. Everyone climbed onto the snow and ice, joking and laughing, and made snowballs in July! We took some souvenir pictures, and caught some of the dripping melt water in our bottles. The little pocket thermometer in my PFD showed that the river's temperature, which had been a cold 9°C (48° F) at the start of Push-Pull Creek, had now fallen by two degrees to only 7°C (45° F). This was very cold water!

After playing on the icefield we paddled on, but soon the weather closed in. A light rain started, and increased as we approached a narrowing in Black Feather Creek. Our map showed that the river was about to be bordered by low cliffs. This would immediately be followed by a long section of rapids. We pulled over on river-left just before the narrows, and got out on a large open shore gravel bar. Otto took a quick look around, and made the logical and welcome call: we would stop here for the night.

While the temperature dropped and things got wetter, we set up our first Mountain River camp. As soon as Kevin and I had our tent pitched I went inside and put on my sweater and new waterproof coral paddling jacket. I also switched hats to my bright lemon yellow Sou'wester. This great, soft plastic rain hat is lined with cozy padding for warmth. Also, its wide brim, being longer at the back than at the front, makes rainwater pour off over the back of my PFD, instead of down my neck.

From our camp, surrounded by millions of glistening, coloured pebbles and rocks, we could see all the way back upriver to the icefield, and beyond, towards the headwaters area and the mountains that surrounded Willow Handle Lake. Bright graceful heads of pink fireweed carpeted large sections of our camp area, scattered throughout the round stones. These lovely blooms were on considerably shorter stems than we were used to at home. Perhaps this was a case of "northern scale," where the harsher conditions and shorter growing season produce lower, smaller, more brilliant blooms. They seemed to have an added luminosity in the clean, damp air, and their light scent combined with the sweet smell of black spruce from the hillside, produced a wonderfully intoxicating blend.

Sprinkled among the flowers and rocks were our four colourful nylon tents. Tent partners had been intentionally kept different than paddling partners, to give a little variety. So I was tenting with Kevin instead of Roger, Brian was tenting with Otto instead of Paddy, and Paddy was tenting with Roger instead of Brian. Bert and Odile, husband and wife, of course stayed together in their own tent.

As we did throughout most of the trip, after setting up our own tents, we all pitched the large group tarp by our big, blue food barrels. Then we built a small fire in our movable, wood burning "environmental stove," under the edge of the tarp. This wonderful, collapsible firebox invention is roughly 43 x 23 x 23 cm when set up. It has a bottom, two sides and an end, all made of sheet metal. A strong grill forms the top, and the box is open on one end, for loading wood, and air. A stove like this uses smaller sticks, and burns considerably less wood than an open campfire, yet it still puts out great heat for cooking and warmth. When set up on top of two small logs, it leaves no blackened rocks or fire pit behind: no trace. It can also easily be turned to maximize the airflow, or can even be lifted and completely relocated while still burning, simply by picking it up using the two logs underneath.

Away from the tent area, we set up our kitchen and eating area under the big tarp, complete with an upside-down canoe for a table, to hold all the fixings. Then we relaxed. The sweet smelling woodsmoke drifted up lazily from the edges of the tarp into the wet air, as we laughed and told stories for hours.

It was well after midnight by the time we finished dinner, yet still light. With gentle rain continuing, we finally drifted off to our tents around 2:00 a.m.: a late day's end following a late start twelve hours earlier back at Willow Handle. Everyone hoped for better weather in the morning.

3

Healing doesn't happen all at once: it takes time. Often, it seems there's no healing going on.

I was being healed of the city, of machines, and the human-centered world. I was shown there are places where nature's elements – which always rule, everywhere and all the time, whether we are aware or not – are inescapably right in your face, in your nose, in your ears, and on your skin.

There's no denying the stark harshness of the wild, but right alongside is a profound tenderness that endures.

———•◦•———

Upriver view, camp, Day 3

– charcoal and conté sketch, Phil Weir

We woke to rain again, after rain throughout the night. This time, for warmth and waterproofing, I pulled my blue "core-temp" neoprene shorts on over top of my red poly-prop long-johns. Coming almost to my knees, these snug fitting shorts are like a mini-wetsuit, protecting the core. Combined with the rest of my rain gear, they would help keep me warm, even in cool, wet weather.

The group decided on a no-travel day for this dank Day 3. We would relax, continue catching up from jet lag and altitude adjustments, re-organize the gear, explore a bit, and sleep there again that night. It rained most of the day.

In a lull, I dug out some art supplies from my pack and did two sketches. One was of the view looking downriver, drawn in my little journal. The other, on my larger sketch pad, was of the view looking back upriver, towards the icefield and head-waters. As I sat by myself quietly drawing, I remembered that, for me the process of doing art is like a meditation. Whatever way it might turn out, the product is mainly just a reminder of the place, the process, and inner feelings that I had going on, during those special times set aside from everything else, just doing art.

In the afternoon, outfitted in our full rain gear, some of us hiked around a bit, exploring the area. The view peeking around the bottom corner of the low cliff by the next down-stream bend looked quite promising. We saw that the first long section of great whitewater was indeed coming right up. To get a better look we climbed a small gully and walked along the tops of the cliffs. As expected, the rapids started immediately, and looked like they would be both challenging and fun the next morning: mainly Class Two and Three.

In the moving-water class system, Class One runs are pretty straightforward, with no mandatory manoeuvres. Class Two are more difficult and involve one or more "must do" moves at some point. Class Three sections are the most challenging, and have even more required moves, often in difficult loca-tions with no room for error. They're supposed to be the upper limit of what open canoes like ours can safely navigate. Class Four is the limit for kayaks or covered boats, and can also be done in a raft. Mortal paddlers in open canoes theoretically can't successfully run Class Four, although it does sometimes happen, through skill or by accident. The rating level of any rapid can also be increased by a half or a full class by vari-ables like changing water conditions, weather, new hazards, or remoteness. But on this no-travel day, there would be no running rapids for us.

The camp duties were getting sorted. Like most groups of trippers, we had organized the main tasks into a duty roster. This makes it easier to get everything done efficiently, and ensures that at least once in a while every person gets a day off. In Norman Wells each of us had been given a laminated copy.

For my first duty I got to make the latrine. I located this up a lovely slope, a couple of hundred metres inland from camp. This glorious spot was surrounded by wildflowers and spectacular panoramic views of the mountains and river; a gorgeous place to stop and sit at any time. After digging a shallow hole in the moss and earth, and positioning a small log across it for balance, I hung a red throw-bag from a bush to flag the spot for the others. Visitors would bring their own t.p.

We enjoyed lazy layover day meals, and spent hours chatting and laughing under the big tarp, watching the little curling waterspouts spill off the corners. We also learned to avoid being doused by the built-up bucketful that would occasionally dump off one side. Our spirits were high despite the rain. Everyone was excited to begin running rapids the next day.

In late afternoon, I got my side of our tent better organized, then lay back and relaxed on my sleeping bag and thin Therm-a-Rest air mattress. My camp pillow was made from a pillowcase stuffed with clothes, which I propped on top of my PFD. Gazing sleepily up at the tent, I let my mind drift around through our fly-in, my solo on Willow Handle, the beginning of Push-Pull Creek, the icefield, the vastness and beauty everywhere we turned, the many laughs with Roger, the fabulous paddling.

My thoughts also floated back home. Already I was missing my wife Jill, our daughter Jody (14), and our two sons Daniel (9) and Patrick (almost 4). Our wonderful family had spent many years camping and tripping together, but for this trip I was on my own. I spent a while looking over my collection of small photos. No matter how far away, I find that those I love are somehow still with me whenever I travel. My family had cared about me enough to give their blessings for this adventure. They knew what I loved and needed to do, and I loved them so much that I wished they could be with me. There would be many stories to share later.

After looking at their pictures I sorted my big turquoise canoe pack, reminding myself of its contents, while also trying to get it into the most efficient order. I had lined the tough, single-opening 70 litre bag with a second heavy-duty drybag. Both these inner and outer sacks have backpack carry straps, and could be used as separate packs. However each has a weakness. If used individually, the lemon yellow inner drybag, made of flexible urethane, nylon and threaded webbing, is completely waterproof; but it's not very resistant to a puncture from a sharp object, such as being set down on a pointed rock or stick. This is an unacceptable risk on a trip like this. On the other hand, my outer turquoise canoe pack is very puncture resistant, being made of much more rugged nylon backpack material. But unfortunately it's not waterproof. When the two bags are combined, the yellow inside the turquoise, the result is a canoe pack that is both rugged and waterproof. As long as I always remember to properly roll and clip the tops of both the inner and outer bags, and tighten all of their straps, then my big pack is theoretically fully submersible, even if bobbing down a river or pinned under the surface. This is important, since it holds nearly all my things.

I had sorted and repacked quickly once before, back at Willow Handle, but this time, down at the very bottom, I was surprised to find a sealed envelope with what felt like a card inside. Jill must have secretly slipped it in back at home. This brought me a warm smile. Such a long way apart, we were still connected. I decided to save it for some special time later, and didn't open it.

4

I have been given the gifts of humility, optimism, and faith in life.

———— • ————

Happy fourth birthday Patrick! It has been such a very hard couple of days for me and all of us since I last wrote in my journal on that layover day.

Over the miles I think of you and Daniel and Jody, together with Jill on this your special day and I wish, I really wish, I was there with you. Summer camp will be done for Jody and Daniel by now, and the family reunited except for me. I look at my little photos of your smiling faces and almost cry I miss you so, though at the same time you make me feel better.

Saturday, our Day 4, was an extremely frightening and difficult day. After getting up at 7:30 we ate, packed, loaded the boats, and took a couple of group pictures. Feeling well prepared after our day without travelling, we launched at

10:30 and continued downriver on fast-flowing Black Feather Creek. As expected, the three kilometre stretch right after camp was excellent whitewater. Though not a full canyon, the cliff banks were several metres high on both sides in sections, and the runs twisty and fast. While paddling those beautiful Class Two and Three rapids we all brushed up on our skills.

Unfortunately, only an hour after launching, just as we were approaching a lovely little chasm that our guide friends had told about, it started to rain hard again. In a lull we ran the narrow channel, which was lined with low, multi-layered sedimentary rock cliffs. These would probably have been light grey if dry, but with all the wet they looked almost black. We named the place "the mini-canyon" or "the not-a-canyon." Paddling through it was great fun, but how much more gorgeous it would be some day to see in the sunshine.

There was one difficult section near the beginning where we all got out on river-right and scouted from a high rock ledge. The river made a quick drop of about a metre on an abrupt narrow bend to the left. Almost immediately there was a sheer cliff face waiting, slam ahead. To avoid ramming into the wall it was mandatory to make a steady ride over the drop, followed by an immediate sharp left. Roger and I went first and manoeuvred it well. Otto and Kevin came second this time, but somehow got spun around backwards during the approach, and had to run the small chute in reverse. They did it with style and grace, as if they had planned it that way. Our other two boats made it just fine.

Though not described in our notes as a canyon, the "not-a-canyon" definitely is one. The narrow cut appears to be located on a fault line. After the first quick drop and bend, the deep, fast channel flows through a beautiful 10 metre wide gap in the 15 metre high gorge. As we floated along through the next kilometre of bending cliffs, the gap increased to 12 metres and the walls rose to 20, before eventually lowering on both sides and widening out to the flood plain.

Once the canyon had opened, some of us turned our canoes around and practiced doing front ferries and back ferries in the current. In the front ferry manoeuvre the canoe is turned to face upstream. Then, while under continuous forward paddling power, the nose is angled slightly into the current and the boat tilted just a little, to the side that one is heading towards. When this combination of angle, motion, and tilt are just right, the moving water pushes the boat laterally across the river, without it travelling upstream or downstream. Done well, the canoe moves quickly straight across, perpendicular to the current, something like a ferry boat. I think it's called a front ferry because the front of the canoe is facing upstream, facing the oncoming current, and it's the front of this ferry that leads as it gets pushed across. The back ferry is the backwards version of the same thing, leading with the stern, like dancing backwards. Together these two manoeuvres are great methods for sliding across a fast river. They are also essential at times.

At around 1:00 p.m., just before we broke for lunch, the rain began pelting down hard once more. I switched hats, donning my Sou'wester, as I had done several times on these chilly, wet days. After tying it on securely, I clipped the chinstrap of my dripping Tilly to the stern thwart in front of me for safe keeping. We all hunkered down, just getting through.

It seemed like it had been dismal, dank weather now for far too long, off and on for three days, and also for at least part of our fly-in day. Chatting glumly as we ate standing in the downpour, we began wondering out loud just how many additional days in a row it might have already rained around here before our group arrived at Willow Handle. Spirits had become subdued.

After our melancholy riverside lunch, and in deteriorating visibility from more driving sheets of rain, we set off again, zooming down around a dozen fast S-bends. With the present deluge, plus who knows how many other days of runoff waters pumping its flow, the current was racing and strong: a swift, swollen, cold river, charging along as if locked on fast-forward. In hindsight, we definitely should have pulled over, stopped, found somewhere, anywhere to camp, and waited out the bad weather. We should have seen it coming. But, perhaps because we had already waited out an extra weather day, we didn't stop. We sped on.

Otto and Kevin were lead boat, Roger and I second, Odile and Bert third, and Brian and Pat fourth. Although things had been happening at a fast, tense pace, we were all doing really well, skillfully navigating the big whitewater, the twists and turns, the drops and rocks. But in a few strokes, just one fast bend in the river, everything changed. Suddenly we were in huge trouble.

The zigzagging escalator had taken our lead boat down around bends and out of sight somewhere ahead in the pelting rain. The river's pitch and speed had increased as it narrowed and dropped through the steep mountainsides, until Roger and I were going full tilt. The rain stung our faces as we squinted to see ahead. We sped around a large, tight bend to the right, with very big haystacks in the middle of the river, bigger than we could safely paddle through. To avoid being swamped, we were riding a bit to the left of centre of the main high-speed current and waves. This was putting us on the mid-outside of the curve. But the outside of a steep, blind, fast corner is not a good place to be on a whitewater river.

The sweeping current was trying to push us further towards the left shore. We could see large rocks coming up there, and so tried to power our way back over further to the right, towards the centre of the river. We were using a strong back ferry, working together, leading with our canoe's rear end, the way we had just done on a few bends in the previous minutes. While pushing hard with our back-paddling, steering, and carefully tilting slightly to the right, we tried to let the river's power push us across, towards the centre, where there were still lots of big frightening waves, but at least no rocks.

This time the current was too fast, too powerful. Trying with all our strength, we just couldn't get our stern over to the right far enough, fast enough, into the edge of those popping haystacks. More importantly we couldn't avoid the big black rock coming up fast in front of us on river-left, about three metres out from shore. From our furious back-paddling and attempted angled sideways motion, our boat was almost completely stopped in its tracks in the churning current when we actually reached that rock.

However, in this case "almost" was definitely not good enough. Our canoe was neither fully stopped, nor over to the right quite far enough to miss touching. Just another moment, maybe three or four more powerful strokes; who knows, fifteen centimetres and we would have cleared it. But there were no more moments for us to somehow paddle harder, no more sideways movement to let us skim past the edge of that rock. We tried our best, but just didn't make it. With large waves heaving directly beside the right gunwale of our open canoe, our nose gently bumped into that memorable black rock – not very hard, but hard enough.

There was no sound from the impact that I could hear over the river's jet engine roar as now this whole frame by frame scene became permanently engraved in slow motion in my memory. Our canoe stopped dead. But the thundering current didn't slow at all. Immediately, huge amounts of water surged in over the top of the right gunwale, flooding the boat in a heartbeat, while simultaneously slamming us broadside against the rock. In the same instant, poor Roger was thrown right out the front of the canoe, pitched into the main haystack current and…he was gone!

In one more moment the canoe's right side rolled down heavily, lumbering deep into the river as the whole boat filled with water faster than if it were hit with a fire hose. The weight and force of the water made the hull start to buckle and breach, with the gunwales facing upstream, wide open to the full intensity of the current, in the worst possible direction. I don't know if it made a groan as it went under, but I did. I knew I had only seconds to prevent myself from falling into that deep, rushing river. There was only one way: I had to go, and go fast! I would have to try to climb out and up, up onto the rock.

With adrenaline racing to the max and a truly desperate feeling, I reached up on the hard wet surface, groping with my left hand, still gripping the stern thwart with my right. Somehow I found a way to hold on to the rock. Then like a big lizard from the deep, I let go of my boat and crawled hand-over-hand, out of the flooded stern, my sinking ship. Somehow around this time I also lost the Grey Owl paddle from my hand, but I can't remember how. It was just gone. No partner, no boat, no paddle! At the very moment that my last foot left the boat, she crumpled even more, wrapping solidly around the face of that rock, aluminum thwarts buckling, plastic hull flattening. The gear started washing out. Our canoe was wrecked in seconds, just like that!

All I could hear was the roar of whitewater. I had found a shaky refuge for now on the very rock we had wrecked upon. I scrambled to crouch, then slowly, carefully, stood up on the slippery top. It was rectangular, only about a metre by a metre and a half. As carefully as possible I began grabbing and unclipping the big tethered food barrel, the packs and other gear, hauling them out of the water, up onto the rock with me. Thank goodness we had clipped them in! Icy water poured over the bent-backwards canoe and the rock below me, and spewed like fountains over my collection of gear, and my feet and ankles.

This was not a safe place to stay! Things could change very fast – they already had. Besides, the salvaged gear now almost completely covered the top of the rock, my tiny base. I had barely anywhere left to stand. Fortunately, the river had another slightly smaller flat boulder just behind and below the first. It was within careful stepping distance for me. Although surges still splashed it, there was less water washing across. The top looked fairly level, being only slightly tilted in the upriver direction. I cautiously took a giant step backwards and sideways, and landed standing on the second rock, still facing upriver.

The full force of the water continued to pound directly at me, and on either side. Though still in tremendous danger, I felt a bit safer the moment I had gotten out of the boat and onto the first rock, and still more secure when I was able to stand instead of crawl. Now, I stood on my second rock base. Good! Progress was happening. I was still in great danger, but everything is relative. In peril, small gains mean a lot.

Both ends of the wrecked canoe now gushed like geysers. Only an arm's length away on my left the deep main current thundered past with those big, cold haystacks. Far across them, over many metres of fast water, was the far shore, much too far to get to. Behind me, a simple slip of my foot away, waited the long, dangerous swim that had taken my partner. I had to maintain focus, keep positive. The closest shore, on river-left, was roughly three metres away from where I stood on the rock – too far to jump. The stern end of the canoe, which was turned completely sideways, with its open side being pummelled by the current, bobbed and waved sporadically. Between the stern tip of the boat and the huge boulders on shore poured a deep fast channel, too deep and fast to wade or swim. I had only my little rock base. But at least I had that. The driving rain kept up and icy river water still rushed over my feet. I thought for a moment of exactly where I was, and I knew: I was alone.

As soon as I climbed out of the boat I had immediately put the whistle, tied by a short string to my PFD, between my teeth, and blasted away with three whistles, three whistles, over and over, meaning, "Emergency!" or "Dump!" While doing this I had watched helplessly as my friend was swept far away, floating downstream at high-speed, his head sometimes bobbing under, trying but unable to get to shore – and I knew more friends were coming! I kept up the blowing, over the roar of the whitewater surrounding me, hoping desperately that Otto and Kevin would hear my signal downriver, and somehow help Roger. At the same time I was frantic that our two approaching upriver boats must hear my whistles, and be able to get themselves quickly and safely to shore, before they too got to where I was, and hit this rock.

Mercifully, just as Roger was about to go out of sight about half a kilometre down on a bend to the left, I saw that he had managed to stop himself, get to shore, and crawl out. Thank God! Then I turned back around, facing upriver and the wreck once more. As water spewed out of it, and over top of it, I kept blasting the emergency signal as hard as I could.

Our canoe's tether rope was holding for now, but was under tremendous strain and might snap at any time. Worse, the whole canoe could perhaps move, lurch in a sudden surge, wash over both the first and second rocks, crush me, pin me, or pitch me into the deep. Black thoughts shot though me, but also hopeful thoughts. The winning inner voices told me, "One thing at a time! What is the most important thing to do this exact second?" And also, "Worry about that later!" Nevertheless, flash fears abounded as I worked at top speed between the two rocks, hauling as much gear as I could onto my little second base. With each piece pulled to safety and unclipped, my hopes increased and despair was put on hold for a few more seconds.

Some items, like our tough plastic Pelican video camera case, were fastened below the waterline to the submerged boat, and I couldn't reach them. These things flailed about like flags in a hurricane under the surface, bashing repeatedly against the rock and the boat. At least I had most of the big items.

Thank goodness our other two boats did hear my whistles, and were able to make successful emergency landings just upriver. This must have required excellent fast manoeuvring. Their skills and quick actions meant that I would have no company on that rock. Time is hard to measure in a crisis, but in what seemed like less than 20 minutes, the others had hiked from their landed boats down along the scree-covered, mountainside shore, to the steep section nearest me. The support of friends is never more welcome than when the going is roughest. The instant I glimpsed them coming in the distance I was filled with relief.

With worry and urgency on every face, the four of them now stood on the jumble of shore boulders directly opposite me. We shouted information back and forth. Over the roar, and with several repetitions for clarity, they became more fully aware of the entire situation. They also quickly threw ropes and biners until I had grabbed one and clipped myself securely around the waist, with them on the other end. I made sure this wasn't fastened with a slip knot, so I wouldn't be throttled around my waist if they had to haul me in. With more tossed ropes I moved back and forth between the two rocks clipping parts of the boat as best I could. Then I started attaching the packs and gear to their other lines and sending them over. The situation was improving again.

By this time Roger had fought off the early stages of hypothermia and scrambled his way back up the shore to be as close as possible to me. Thank God he was OK! Later he would say, "And thank my mother's prayers!" Badly shaken, but unhurt and still clutching his paddle, he proceeded to help with the rescue. What an amazing trooper! I'm not sure if he actually stared at me, sent me a firm grin, and shouted, "Don't worry partner!" but it sure felt like it. He gave me faith.

In the first few moments after the group arrived I lost my trusty PFD knife. I had pulled it from its fastener and was using it to free gear when I foolishly put it down on a pack for just a second. Like a living thing, the river instantly surged, washed over it, and took it away. Gone! "Rookie mistake!" Roger said later, and he was right.

This was an error not to be repeated, but still I urgently needed to have a knife to cut the tether line loose under the water, and free the remaining submerged gear. The group sent out Roger's knife on a rope, and I could finally carefully kneel and reach deep under the surface of the cold rushing water with both hands and cut the line. The hand without the knife pulled up the freed video camera case. I tied it to a rope and sent it over. This time, to be sure not to lose it, I kept Roger's knife clenched firmly between my teeth at all times when not in use, just like in the movies. Next the heavy food barrel went across to the shore crew, then Roger's big canoe pack, then mine, the camera tripod, Roger's small daypack, and finally my spare Mohawk aluminum paddle.

Still the icy water surged and splashed, rushing sometimes 15 centimetres above my feet, which were now quite cold despite the neoprene bootie socks. Rain continued to pour off the back of my Sou'wester as I tried to make sure that I had done all I could to secure the boat with shore ropes. After what seemed like an hour, working with careful small steps on the slippery tops of the two rocks, it was time for me to try and get to shore. I had done all I could out there. Two or three lines were firmly attached to our canoe, and had been secured on land. As much gear as I could salvage was now across.

Some of my worries had subsided but new ones had developed. I had become increasingly cold, wet, and tired. I knew about the dangers of hypothermia, which surely had begun: about the growing risk of errors in judgement and self-assessment; the increasing muscle impairment and lack of coordination; the heightened possibilities of sudden slips, cold immersions, concussions, foot entrapment, broken bones – and of drowning.

I remembered my promise to Jill before the trip: that I would return safe to her and the kids. As I drew up all my courage and strength, I inwardly vowed to keep that promise.

Unknown to us at the time, five or six quick bends further down the river, Kevin and Otto had themselves come close to capsizing by a cliff, after going over a ledge. But they stayed upright. With their canoe almost full of sloshing water, they quickly pulled over on river-left. Moments after hopping out, and while still working to bail, they heard emergency whistle signals. These had perhaps come from Roger, who had just crawled out onto land upriver a couple of bends, or maybe they heard some of mine from further upriver.

Jumping into action they stood watching the river like hawks, rescue throwbags in hand, ready to toss, as a couple of tense minutes ticked by. No people or boats floated down. They knew what this meant: something very serious must have happened upriver. And the situation was urgent. With inner red lights flashing, they ferried over to the river-right bank, where the land was a little lower and it was easier to walk. Quickly securing their canoe, they began hiking on-the-double up the rivershore to help. I was just about to leave the rock when the two of them arrived on the far shore immediately across the river from the rest of us.

It had not been an easy hike. Their route had started with a moderate climb, and the rest had been uneven and rocky. Most unfortunately, in their rush up the jumble of wet shore boulders and rough scree, Otto had stumbled and cut his left shin badly on a sharp rock. He was bleeding. The deep four centimetre long gash went right to his bone. Kevin helped him finish the hike to the point opposite us, and now they were both there, calling to us across the roar. They were getting the news, and so were we.

After a few minutes of hollering back and forth, the reality sank in, and all of us, on both sides of the river, understood the full weight of the complete group situation: it was still driving rain, Otto was in need of immediate First Aid, and he and Kevin were on the other side of this fast, dangerous river bend, with their boat downstream. Roger was back, helping with the group, but had experienced a terrifying swim and had come close to drowning. I was still on the rock, just about to try to get to shore. This was one more of those pivotal moments, a reference point forever in my life.

There was no delaying. It was time to permanently leave the second rock, my little temporary base, and return one last time to the first one. My plan was that I would gather all my personal inner resources and try to tight-rope walk as far as I dared along the bobbing, unstable, underwater edge of our sideways, pinned canoe. It was dangerous, perhaps not even possible, but clearly my only way to shore. I also knew that if I was going to survive this walk on water, I would have to face my fears head on, keep my confidence and faith unshakable, and have complete focus. My family needed me back home.

It felt like I'd been on that rock for well over an hour when I finally stepped off, towards land and friends. Who knows how long it really was: perhaps a lifetime.

Holding my shore line tightly for balance, and flexing my knees to ride the bumps and sways, I concentrated on sliding one slow baby-step forward at a time. With each small move-ment the shift made my black plastic gangplank sink deeper, sending more water rushing over my feet and ankles. I eventu-ally reached the point where the waving end of the boat had sunk so low, that I knew it wouldn't be able to hold me if I slid a foot any further. If I ended up falling into that deep fast water, I knew my friends would pull me out with the shore line as fast as they could, but not before the current would pummel me downstream some distance, smashing me into the big shore boulders, some of which looked pretty sharp. How long might I be under? No, I would have to pull hard on their rope, and do a huge leap.

Summoning body, mind and spirit I did what felt like an Olympic-class standing broad jump, and lunged that final distance to shore, while the rescuers helped pull me across. To land firmly in the arms of friends, on solid ground, after facing such danger was a tremendous joy. Thank God I was ashore and unhurt! Roger was ashore and unhurt! And, we had recovered most of the gear! But, with 13 days of canoe travel still ahead to get to the Mackenzie River, our boat was a horrible mess.

In my mind I kept hearing a recording of Bill Mason's voice speaking words from his great instructional canoeing movie *Path of the Paddle*. Although he says it only once in the film, in my brain I heard it over and over: "A canoe in this position is irretrievable. A canoe in this position is irretrievable. A canoe in this position is…"

Despite everything I felt extremely lucky, even blessed. The river had taken our boat, but not our lives, or our health. In coming so close to dying I felt I had been given a new life. What would I do with it? A truly humbling, life-altering experience was in process, and I resolved to learn and grow from this turning point.

But I would figure all that out later, because right now Otto needed our help.

5

The river gave me my life back.

———— ◆ ————

My main gear lost was the new wooden Grey Owl paddle, and my old green daypack loaded with stuff, including my SLR camera, my journal of our first three days, and one of my two sketches from our first river camp. Fortunately I hadn't lost my spare aluminum Mohawk paddle, a favourite that I had paddled with for many years. But Roger's spare aluminum one, provided by the outfitter, was gone. My water bottle, binered to the stern thwart, didn't come out, nor did my single-use fishing rod. By now all of these were washed away, smashed, or scattered on the riverbed somewhere downstream from the wrecked canoe, lost to the river. Saddest of all, my heart felt crushed knowing that Jill's card was gone. I had put it in my little daypack, to save for later, but never had the chance to read it. I want her to tell me what it said when I get home.

After doing our best to secure the lines that were attached to the canoe to big shore boulders, and making sure that the salvaged gear was safely away from the water's edge, we all rushed upstream along the steep hillside to the small shore gravel bar where our third and fourth boats had made their emergency landings. This was the only semi-level space in the entire area. It now became our temporary work base.

To bring Otto and Kevin across to our side required extremely careful front ferrying. Because Odile had more paddling experience in big whitewater, she would temporarily take Brian's place in the bow of Pat's boat. In the continuing rain we quickly unloaded all the gear from their canoe, then the two of them got in and, with the rest of us watching anxiously, bravely paddled the empty boat across the river to pick them up. Almost immediately they had to pass through the same frightening haystacks which had worried Roger and I so much, but their front ferry worked a lot better than our back ferry had. Ever-mindful that they were only seconds upriver from the rock with our pinned boat, Pat and Odile were extremely cautious and professional. Since the current was too strong to allow safe passage with all four people in one canoe, they had to make two trips, bringing one passenger over at a time. Otto came first, then Kevin. Later Pat and Odile went across the river a third time, and got the big packs, barrel and other gear, which they hiked up from Otto and Kevin's downstream boat. Now we were eight back together again on the gravel bar on river-left, and this was a big relief, despite our situation.

Everyone immediately got to work trying to help Otto. There was no shelter or even a small protected area on the shore gravel bar to get him out of the rain. With no branches or bushes available to hold up a tarp, we had to improvise. A circle of five lifted the big group tarp, using only their arms above their heads. This created a large temporary umbrella. They held it steadily, shielding us, while underneath Odile and I gave Otto emergency First Aid.

The group worked as a unit as his leg was elevated, the deep shin gash washed with hydrogen peroxide, covered with antibiotic cream, pulled together with three butterfly stitch band-aids, protected with a sterile gauze pad, then held in place with a tensor bandage. Topping it all off, in true camper style, the entire area was covered with duct tape, to keep it sealed and waterproof. It was quick and rough, but Otto was immediately in much better shape.

We then rushed about, setting up an emergency camp. A wet fire was lit, and a more permanent big tarp erected using ropes and also sticks found further up the shore. I was in medium hypothermia and shock from everything, and warmed myself by the fire as our tent was set up. Then I went and changed into dry clothes. Thank goodness the inside of my pack was still dry. I came back to the fire, warmed myself more thoroughly and ate quietly. Roger did the same. Both of us were stunned, quiet and pensive. It sank in further, just how close we had come to disaster. Although the words were unspoken, we both knew we could have died.

Every one of us was shaken as we quietly pieced together a rough camp. We were just upriver from the pinned boat. What would we do now? Each person had their own thoughts, but for a long time there was very little talking. Besides the wrecked canoe, we worried about the possibility of the river rising further in the night due to the continuing rain. We had all heard stories of how, in mountain valleys a river can change levels quickly due to rapid runoff, especially from bare slopes like these.

To try to keep an eye on possible changes in the river level, I built what I called a rough "weir," consisting of six marker sticks. The base of each stick was held in place by a mound of pebbles, so it stood up straight. Each was placed about a "ground foot" or 30 centimetres from the other, moving inland, away from the water's edge. The base of the first stick touched the edge of the water, marking the present water level and location of the shoreline. If the water rose, reaching successive sticks, this would demonstrate the amount of increased river level. If it rose all the way to stick number six, we would have to move our camp to the slightly higher, and very rocky main bank. There, we would have to set up somehow in a jumble of big rocks, below a cliff. This was not a comfortable thought, especially in the rain. Neither location was a safe place to camp, but there were no other options.

After the first session of group discussions around the fire, I went to our tent at 9:00 exhausted, while the others stayed up talking. But I couldn't get to sleep, thinking of Roger floating downstream, of our ruined boat, of being on that rock, and of what on earth will we do now. Combined with the residual adrenaline pumping through me, this made for a very fitful couple of hours napping. I felt crushed, believing I was fully responsible, that I had risked my friend's life, endangered everyone, and ruined the group's trip. I had done my very best, but it just wasn't good enough. The whippings we give ourselves are far worse than any others. Hindsight can help us avoid repeating problems in the future, but it was no help to me that night. Our boat was totalled.

Thankfully I managed to avoid the deepest pit of despair, but I did spend a lot of time in guilt, sadness, self-deprecation, shame, doubt, and fear. I told myself that I loved my wife and kids; that somehow I would get back to them, get back home. I knew I would, but I didn't know how. I thought of Patrick, and hoped he had had a good fourth birthday, back in Ottawa.

At midnight, for some reason I woke up abruptly. I sat up and looked out our tent door flap, to see how things were looking, and was shocked to see the edge of the river lapping only 15 centimetres from our tent! My feet were almost in it! I jumped up in alarm. Kevin and I immediately roused everyone. The group had to bug-out quickly: that is, we had to break our emergency camp, and move everything over to the main river-left bank. All six of my marker sticks were gone! Every one of them had floated away!

Thank goodness the rain stopped for a short time while we moved. The river had risen so high in just a few hours that our crescent shaped gravel bar was no longer attached to the mainland. It had become an island! It was also probably still shrinking, since we had every reason to believe the river was still rising. There was now a fast flowing, two metre wide channel of river water between us and the mainland! We had to load our two boats up several times, and float everything across.

The mainland shore was no welcoming place. It consisted of a rough jumble of large boulders and sharp scree at the base of a tall, steep cliff. Going up or down the shore was no better. The broad side of the cliff also had talus fans of loose rock, which indicated recent landslides. The present weather conditions surely didn't add to their stability. However, once moved, at least we were on the mainland, and the area was significantly higher than the river level. By 2:00 a.m. our scrambled base relocation was complete. Exhausted, and now with even more worries, we all went back to bed, just as the rain started up once more.

Our physical situation now was that we were very roughly camped, on unlevel ground, under a rocky cliff, in the rain. I don't think I slept a total of two hours after that. Lying restless and fretful, I listened as many little rocks and not-so-little boulders, apparently loosened by the rain, came clicking, clacking, tumbling, and sometimes crashing down the cliff-side. A couple sounded as if they were falling from somewhere almost directly above. I had visions of a boulder suddenly smashing through our tent, or a rockslide burying us alive. Above all I kept thinking, "I wish, I wish I was with you guys: my love, my kids. I've got to get back there with you." I had several crying times, even said some prayers.

I tried to think of ideas. In the semi-dark of that wet night, there didn't seem to be many. If we weren't able to get the boat off, one option that the group had tossed around by the fire earlier was for Roger and I to wait here at our emergency camp, while the rest complete the journey in our three remaining good boats. They could then arrange for a rescue, and we could perhaps get flown out by chopper evacuation, sent from Norman Wells. This wasn't a popular idea, but was our worst case scenario. I thought of what it might be like for the two of us to stay here for two weeks, or longer, waiting. We were probably out of helicopter range anyway.

On the more positive side, I thought that maybe, just maybe, there might be a way to get our boat off of that rock, and out of the river. Maybe it was retrievable somehow. If we did get it out, then maybe we could fix it up to be reasonably seaworthy. And then…then maybe we could float out in it. We could finish our trip.

Maybe. But how? As the clicking and clacking of tumbling stones continued all around our tent, finally exhaustion overcame me. I could only resolve to wait, and see what the morning would bring.

6

The dangerous times, and also the quiet times, made me realize what my true priorities are: after survival comes my family. It sank in deeply how blessed I am to have a family to come back to.

———— •·•————

When we got up the next day the first thing we did was hike down the shore to look at the canoe. Walking along I was told that, while I lay in my tent last night, before the others had gone to bed the first time, they had come to a consensus. The only way to get the boat off the rock was to first wait for the rains to end, so the river would stop going up. Then, provided the pinned canoe was unchanged when the waters eventually went down a bit, we could try to build an upstream diversionary dam, using rocks from the steep hillside beside the wreck. A makeshift dam might be able to deflect the main current enough to relieve some of the pressure on the boat. Maybe then we would be able to pull her off.

These tactics were desperate measures, but what else could we do? Everyone knew that, even if this worked, we still had no way of knowing whether whatever we might pull out of the river would be in any way repairable. For several reasons we didn't want to split the group and send some ahead, probably thirteen days ahead, for help, but this option was still reserved as the last resort. Confused and worried, the others had gone to bed. Then the river had risen higher, and forced our middle of the night camp relocation.

On this drizzly "morning after," when we got to the wreck site and looked down, we were devastated. The river had swollen much higher than yesterday, even higher than late last night during our bug-out. Our taut lines now dove down deep into the water and utterly disappeared! The boat was gone! Even the rock she was pinned on was gone! Sometime in the night our canoe had vanished beneath the rising surface.

We stared dumbfounded at the roaring water. The tension on the ropes told us there must still be something attached down there, but we could only imagine the shape it would be in. Only a small ripple remained on the surface to show where the boat, or some part of it, was still pinned; that, and those plunging lines.

My nightmare black thoughts returned full force. Last night we had known we were in big trouble. Now, in the dull light of morning, overwhelmed by the vision of the loss of even the remains of our boat, everyone knew our troubles were much worse. We stood huddled, stunned, looking down at the river. No one spoke as it sank in. We shook our heads, and kept them low.

It was a very quiet breakfast fire. The drizzle turned into rain. Next to my time on the rock, this early morning was my personal darkest time. My heart ached. I was filled with thoughts that were black and lonely. More than ever I felt the complete responsibility for what had happened. It was my fault, all my fault. There would be no absolution, no redemption, no recovery. Once again I whipped myself for not being stronger, smarter, more skilful, for not somehow doing more, for not being a better man. Sitting alone, away from the others, crying inside, I stared with unfocussed eyes at the grey, thundering water. Despair was winning.

At this exact darkest personal moment, when things were so very grim, my friends came through. I looked up from my sadness and saw these people, all of whom I had put at such great risk, simply get up and walk over to that hillside. One by one: Kevin, Roger, Bert, Brian, and the others went to the slope just upriver from the wreck. Slowly, carefully, deliberately, they began rolling rocks down. They were starting to make the dam! True heroes! I shook off my blackness, got up, walked over and helped. We would build a dam! And get her off!

The shore a few metres upriver from the wreck was almost a sheer drop-off, but our dam had to be located there. Also, the bed of the river at that particular spot was unfortunately quite deep: perhaps five metres. This was not an easy or safe place to work, but this big hole would need to be filled if we hoped to deflect the current. We began rolling and dropping boulders from the adjacent steep hillside into the deep water. Crews gradually worked further up the rocky slope, getting more and more boulders, until eventually we were pushing rocks in long production lines from high above. Life jackets were worn at all times in case someone tumbled down the slope into the river. It was slippery, dangerous work. We watched out for each other.

I and some of the others had a few twinges of guilt about altering the river in such a dramatic and disrespectful way, but we knew that the results of our efforts would be temporary, and would be washed away by the next surging flood. This river was mightier than anything we eight travellers could do to alter it for long. It would restore itself.

It was hours before we could see any of our rocks poking into the air just above the surface of the water, as we built our dam slowly out from shore. After several more hours of hard labour we had built it only two metres into the river. This was indeed a very deep hole to fill. But two metres was two metres! Now at least we could solidly stand, where before there was deep rushing water. We had the beginnings of a rescue base.

I forget at exactly what point that great Stan Rogers song came into my head. Perhaps it was when we first started to work on the dam, or soon after. "The Mary Ellen Carter" is a wonderful song which tells the story of a boat that went down, and of her crew who wouldn't let her stay down. They worked for months, going underwater in dive suits, patching and repairing her against all odds, then filling her with air and floating her up, to be on the surface once again. It has lines in it like:

Oh we couldn't leave her there you see to crumble into scale....

And you, to whom adversity has dealt the final blow,
With smiling bastards lying to you everywhere you go,
Turn to and put out all your strength of arm and heart and brain,
And like the Mary Ellen Carter, rise again!

Rise again! Rise again!
Though your heart it be broken or life about to end.
No matter what you've lost! — be it a home, a love, a friend,
Like the Mary Ellen Carter,
Rise again!

"The Mary Ellen Carter" – Stan Rogers (SOCAN)
c p Fogarty's Cove Music 1979. Used by permission.

Thank you Stan Rogers! What a fabulous inspiring song! I started singing it, and teaching it to the others.

We spent all day building our base outwards, working in shifts of four or five. Everyone knew we were out to beat stiff odds, but we worked together and didn't give up. We joked and encouraged each other. Like characters from some Greek myth, we just kept toiling, rolling hundreds of boulders, maybe thousands, down the hillside, always making sure there was no-one below as they fell.

By the end of the day we needed to push, drag and lever the rocks into long pathways or chutes to get them down about 20 metres to the flat top of our dam. We would then muscle them out to the end, and dump them in. It was heartbreaking to watch most of them just disappear under the surface. Sometimes we could hear them bumping away deep. We prayed they weren't tumbling all the way to the boat and hitting it.

Eventually we had built a rough triangle, 4 x 4 x 4 m out into deep water. The all-morning rain decreased to a couple of light showers by early afternoon. We worked right through them. Mercifully, the river level also began dropping gradually. By the time we knocked off and ate dinner the rain had stopped entirely. When I was ready to head to bed, a bunch of us walked over to look down on the spot again. We were heartened to see the river had lowered even further, and was almost down to the level that it had been at the night before. Even more wonderful, our boat had come back into view, the same way it had been just after the wreck! Thankfully it didn't seem to have changed much, except that now we had a solid dam just upriver from it to work from. We could see that the current's strength was indeed beginning to be deflected to the right, and it looked like this was resulting in less water pressure on the wrapped canoe.

If only the weather would improve a bit more and hold, we just might get this boat to rise again! We were extremely weary and aching, but things were looking better. Sleep came much easier in our emergency camp that second night.

———•—•———

7

There were gifts of camaraderie and teamwork, of increased understanding of others, and their strengths and unique traits too.

———•••———

I woke full of hopes, fears and questions. Would the boat be submerged again, or washed away? Would we get it off? If we did, would it be repairable or hopelessly ruined? Everyone knew: one way or another, this day would be pivotal.

We again scouted immediately, before morning coffee. This time we were thrilled to see the boat in pretty much the same condition as we had left her: still in sight, still attached to our ropes, and the ropes secured to big rocks on the shore.

After a quick breakfast we worked all morning, shoving and rolling more boulders, enlarging and strengthening our dam. We had used up most of the available small and medium sized rocks on the first day, and now had to tackle some that were quite massive. A few were almost as big as Roger. Some of us also used long, three metre by ten centimetre spruce poles as levers. We taught ourselves crash courses, learning the proper placement of a lever and fulcrum, the most productive ways of pushing a really heavy rock, and what could be done to reduce friction. It would sometimes take four of us together to slide a single large boulder, bit by bit, to the dropping point.

We knew that besides deflecting the current more, the further out into the river we could get on our dam, the better would be our hauling angle to stand and pull, and therefore the greater our chances of pulling the boat free. Since the river-right shore was at least 18 metres away, and had no strong trees, large boulders, or even any good stable places to stand, no cross-river pulley systems or rescue Z-drags were possible. We knew that the only way to do it was from this side, standing on our dam, working together.

Finally we had built the base out roughly 5.5 x 5.5 x 5.5 m, with a blunt 4 metre outermost edge. The plunging slope of the river was dramatically demonstrated to us by the fact that the water at the top, or upriver side of our dam, was a full vertical metre higher than that on the lower, downriver side. This meant that the river was making a one metre descent in a run of only 5.5 metres, a drop of almost 20 percent.

We were cautiously optimistic. The current was now being deflected well to the right, considerably reducing the water pressure on the canoe. The end closest to shore (the sideways stern that I had walked along) had started to bounce a bit more in the surges and ebbs as it continued to spout water like a fountain. This was a good sign. It was time to try.

After lunch and further discussions of tactics, all of us went to a high point on the hillside and looked down on the boat and dam, doing our final planning. We were full of hope but also dread: this had to work. We talked of where to place spruce logs as levers, of which ropes would need to be pulled first and in what ways, of the importance of not letting the wreck get away from us once we pried it off, and of where exactly we would try to bring her to land.

Everyone would have to shout loudly out there, to be able to hear each other over the constant roar. From the big shore boulders directly beside the wreck, Roger would use a long spruce pole under the end of the boat, and try to lever it a bit to the right, in the upriver direction, towards the dam. A couple of metres upriver Otto, Bert and Brian would manipulate another, much longer, heavier log, as a second lever. At the same time that Roger would be trying to force the sideways stern upriver, against the remaining current, the three prying with the second lever would attempt to also raise it upwards, higher on the rock. This would hopefully relieve even more water pressure from the boat.

Meanwhile a crew of four on the dam would work with the ropes that were tied to the boat, and try to haul the sideways stern further up towards the outer corner of the dam. If it could be pulled up far enough, and away from the rock just a tiny bit, some of the river's rushing water would be able to get underneath the boat, and a surge could allow it to float free, towards the right, the middle of the river.

With grim pride we knew we had prepared as much as we could. I held the sweetgrass tightly in my pocket for a minute. After taking some still photos, we set up the video camera on the hillside, aimed it so that it framed the dam, the rock and the pinned canoe, and pushed Record. We left it running and took our positions. With everyone ready, we began the recovery.

Our dam had done a good job of lessening the pressure on the stern half of the canoe. The initial levering by the two logs worked well. Various combinations of people on the dam we were able to gradually pull the end of the boat up to about a metre away from the lower end of our dam. After this, the largest log lever couldn't do much more. Otto stayed and kept it in place in case of a setback, while Brian and Bert came onto the dam to help pull. The boat was now almost parallel with the force of the current. Many sets of determined hands held ropes. The main line connected to the end of the stern had four people gripping along it, as in a tug-of-war.

From the outermost tip of our base, Kevin pushed on the end of another long spruce pole, leaning his body precariously out over the water, trying to pry the end of the canoe outwards and downriver. The fastest part of the deflected current was flying past on his right hand side like a blur. To prevent him from falling into it and being swept away, Brian held tightly to the back of his brother's life jacket, and also to a rope tied to Kevin's waist. A further backup rope was kept on Brian and tied to shore. Altogether, it seemed like almost every rope and carabiner in the group had been used.

The dam, spruce poles, ropes, biners, calculation, levering, pushing, pulling, and a hell of a lot of great teamwork, finally all paid off. After about four hours in total, she came sliding off that rock! As a rope was carefully untied from shore, Kevin, who was pushing far out over the river on his pole, felt the boat start to move and joyfully shouted, "There she goes!" At 6:50 p.m., slipping off from the rock into the deep water on the right-hand side, and held securely by our ropes, the wrecked boat floated free!

Twisting and bouncing like a giant fishing lure in the main current, we steered her using the lines, down past the rock that had held her pinned for two full days. Carefully easing them out a bit more, we let her slip a metre further downriver, past that second rock, the one where I had stood for so long. As we guided her carefully, the flattened canoe cleared every obstacle. With cheers, whoops and hollers, the group triumphantly hauled her in to the water's edge and safely onto shore. She came to rest on dry land at last! Hallelujah! We got our boat back!

Euphoria raced though everyone in a flood of relief and achievement. Yes, she was crushed, flattened, bent, and looked almost as if a steam-roller had gone over her; and yes she looked like a very large black banana peel with bumps. Most people would see her as just a big piece of junk that could never float again. But we were totally ecstatic, and gave each other enthusiastic high-fives all around. We would work it out. We knew we would.

To our amazement, although flattened, the plastic hull was still whole, without a single hole. It was scraped but not torn. Both the pointed ends were intact. Every one of the aluminum gunwales was bent, creased, or kinked, but none were gone, and none completely ripped through. Our two seats were broken, where they were joined to the hull, but they too were still there. Every thwart and support post was buckled, but all of them still there. Unbelievable! The river had left us all the parts.

She had been wrapped on that rock for 52 hours, under the water for over two full days and nights, pounded by heavy current, rubbed and scraped. But now, there she was, resting with us on land. With good fortune and teamwork, we had made her rise again. Far from being discouraged by her crumpled, battered state, we were elated. We had hope!

As an added bonus, to my delight still tied to it were my Tilley hat, my full water bottle, and also Roger's water bottle. The tattered, clipped in, remains of my old green canvas day-pack were there too, strap and all. The entire contents were gone of course. The current had left behind just a shredded rag. Only my metal spare whistle remained tied to the strap. My canvass Tilly hat, so recently white and new, had turned grey, but it was still there, clipped to the kinked stern thwart by its, now slightly worn, chinstrap. It had been permanently tinted by the river's silt, and had a few nicks and scrapes, but I was quite pleased to have my hat back.

Best of all, the lemonade in my still-full water bottle was wonderfully ice cold, and absolutely delicious. With hugs and hearty high-fives we passed it all the way around, toasting each other. No champagne could have tasted better.

In triumph, our rescue crew manhandled the flattened, black beast up the hillside five metres or so, then across to the flat gravel bar beside camp. When the water level dropped, this area had returned to being dry and attached to shore, and it now again became our work area. Crowding around the treasure, we did a more thorough examination and were delighted to see that it looked like we would indeed be able to fix her!

Working together, we did some careful dancing and stomping around inside the hull, followed by bending and pounding. To everyone's astonishment, after only fifteen minutes she had popped back into reasonably good shape! We couldn't believe it! This was one tough boat! Our earlier concerns about the canoe's heaviness, unusual support features, and strange aesthetics vanished, as we realized that it had survived its ordeal.

With only a bit more work, in less than an hour after hauling it out of the river, our boat had been made basically seaworthy: an amazing resurrection! Roger and I knew for sure now that we would be able to complete our trip in it. Boosted by this knowledge, we all decided to rest for the evening and celebrate. We would complete the last of the detailed repairs in the morning.

What a wonderful time it was! Elated, we again hugged and high-fived each other in camp, and even did some dancing around. We laughed with delight, and tears of pure joy and relief. We also triumphantly gave each other "paddlers' handshakes." This type of solidarity handshake is slightly different from a normal one, and involves the hands holding the fleshy bases of the thumbs, with the thumbs up, and fingers clasped around, forming almost a double fist.

The entire group exhaled in joy. I was so happy that I even bathed in the freezing cold river, sitting in the shallow water at the edge of the gravel bar beside camp. Feeling blessed, I thanked the river. This delightful experience was like a casting off of the last few days' troubles, a purging of worries, a new beginning. I then put on a complete set of clean clothes, which, as any camper knows, is a special occasion on a long trip.

We were such a happy camp that night, feasting on an extra big meal, relaxing around the fire, chatting and laughing loud and long. Bert, or perhaps it was Paddy, magically came up with some whiskey, and kindly shared small cups of cheer with everyone. Still amazed at our luck, we all went over the stories of the recovery. Roger and I were happiest of all. Everyone would be continuing on together.

On the day of our dump, when Otto and Kevin had heard the whistle signals, they immediately began hiking quickly up the river-right shore to help us. Just after they had started, they scrambled up a small rise by the water and found three large feathers from a golden eagle. This was shortly before Otto fell and hurt his leg. The two feathers that Kevin picked up were large, perhaps 20-30 centimetres, and Otto found the largest one, measuring 60 centimetres. It had apparently come from the tip of the eagle's right wing. This was the biggest feather I had ever seen, other than from an ostrich. It was only a bit short of being as long as my arm. Its shaft was as thick as a pen at the base. When I saw these feathers I privately wished I could find one for Daniel. But these things have to come to you when the time is right.

Later, Otto sewed his huge feather solidly alongside his hat, where it flew trailing behind him for about 40 centimetres from his right side. The second feather, still quite big, was given by Kevin to Brian, who also fastened it to his own hat, this time on the left side, and from there it trailed about 30 centimetres. They both looked fabulous.

Earlier today as we all pulled together on the wrapped boat, just before the moment when she floated free, a huge golden eagle had soared way up high, directly above us, in ascending circles. It then glided off silently, disappearing over the canyon wall, heading downriver. With all of the sky to choose from, this eagle had soared directly above us, and it did so right at this crucial time. It was surely a good omen, on this exceptionally good day. We decided to call this place "Eagle Rock."

Tomorrow we would finish our canoe repairs, break camp, and travel on. My thoughts continued to be full of awe and gratitude. We had not only recovered our pinned and battered canoe, but she had come back to us in a condition that allowed us to make her seaworthy again. Despair had transformed into elation. Lying on my back in our tent I prepared for a much more peaceful sleep. I thanked the Great Spirit, the River, the Lord, my good fortune, my lucky stars, fate, the sweetgrass, my own mother's prayers, my family's love; and I especially thanked my friends. Our teamwork, spirit, and luck, had seen us through.

I smiled upwards. We had our canoe back! Otto's leg was healing well. It was cloudy but it wasn't raining. We would continue on together tomorrow; perhaps more slowly, and with greater caution, but we would travel on. I again felt the powerful feeling that I had experienced just after leaping from the rock onto the shore. I felt I had been given a new life. Meegwetch!

Over the next few days I rewrote the contents of my lost journal, and the details of our wreck and recovery, into a new little journal notebook that Kevin kindly gave to me.

8

The river gave us our boat back.

———•◆•———

There were no camp sounds yet, only the river. I thought of the canoe and smiled. It was going to be a good day. Kevin slept on a little longer as I quietly got ready for the new day.

Barely awake, I was sitting up in my sleeping bag, digging down to the very bottom of my canoe pack, looking for something. Suddenly I realized my fingers had touched stiff dry paper! With a zing of electricity my head cleared. It could only be one thing! With a bolt of excitement I reached a little further down, grabbed a corner, and carefully pulled upwards through the jumble of clothes. I could hardly believe it. In my hand was the envelope with Jill's card! It was just as I had last seen it: perfect, safe, dry, hardly even bent. Not lost to the river! My eyes moistened as I realized I would have a second chance to read it after all. It dawned on me that I must have stuck it down there in the bottom of my big pack for safe keeping the night before the wreck. I had not put it, as I had thought, into my little green, now-shredded daypack. How quickly things can change! My faulty memory had caused me grief, but now, joy overcame it all.

After staring at the envelope and fingering the smooth dry parchment for a minute, I slowly opened it. Sitting quietly I slipped the card out. It had wildflowers on the front. I silently read Jill's secret message. We were connected.

She said by the time I read this I would be on the river somewhere, that she would be thinking of me, that she hoped I would be having lots of wonderful adventures, and that I should have a fabulous time. She also said she loved me very much. The last thing she said was that I must come home safe to her and the kids. That part made me cry.

She had written those wonderful words to me way back in Ottawa, before I left, and somehow slipped the card into my pack. Now here I was, finally reading it, so far away, after such difficult days and nights, and after thinking the card was lost to the river. In my mind I said to her, "Yes, I will come home safe my love. I promise I will. – And yes, despite all our difficulties, I will have a wonderful time."

After reading it a few times, I carefully put the card back into the envelope, and stuffed it back into the bottom of my pack. Glowing inside, I finished dressing and got up. What a fabulous start to our "moving on" day.

———•—•———

It took less than an hour for the group to finish repairing the canoe. We used our repair kit, pliers, string, screws, and of course, lots of duct tape and creativity. Spruce log reinforcements were tied under the kinked thwarts and beside the damaged support posts. One of the hollow thwarts was almost broken through, so we smoothed the jagged ends, slid a spruce log inside for reinforcement, then pushed the two ends back together and duct taped the entire joint. A long, thin spruce pole was also tied to the full length of the inside of the bottom of the canoe, reinforcing the existing kinked aluminum piece. We made sure that all loose parts of the seats and thwarts were firmly reattached. No longer a flattened piece of junk, she was now a uniquely rigged, somewhat clunky looking, whitewater canoe. To Roger and I she looked fabulous!

Before leaving, I put on my life jacket and took a last solo walk downriver, along the high shore. I stood quietly for several minutes looking down at Eagle Rock. I had been blessed several times at this place. We had all worked so hard here. I could have died here. Roger could have died. Our boat could have been irretrievable, or irreparable. Severe injuries, and worse, could have happened here. I closed my eyes. When I opened them I looked all around me again, and smiled at how beautiful everything was. Life is good. Every day is a gift.

I took the sweetgrass braid out of the plastic bag in my pocket and burned a bit. The smoke drifted as I listened to the roar and watched the water thunder down the river. "Everything will be alright, but not necessarily how we think." This river would be flowing through these mountains long after we were gone. The steep mountain hillsides, cliffs and wildflowers would also remain. I walked away slowly, feeling very philosophical. I was just a visitor, a nomad passing through. We all were. I was perhaps an especially lucky visitor. Now I was moving on. What had I learned? What would stay with me?

While I was lost in thought above the rock, everyone had no-traced the camping area. The river would also no-trace this area of any remaining record of us. Our puny dam would soon be gone, washed away by the next big storms. Eagle Rock would return to being as it was before. There would be no more pinned canoe, no camp, no people. This rock was really just another rock; and this place, just another bend in a long river. What continued on from our time here would be whatever each of us carried inside.

———◆◆———

The river was calling. So were our four good boats! We finished packing, loaded, and at 10:30 a.m. on the fourth day after we had arrived at this place, we pushed off. Because Otto and Kevin's canoe was still downriver, we had to first carefully shuttle everyone and all of the gear across those haystacks again, using three boats. But on this day, the river was gentler, and flowing lower. We were also rested and calmer, and the skies were only partly cloudy. There was no rain.

During our first few moments back in the canoes we were all nervous, especially me! I felt like someone who had just rolled a car on a remote highway, and it had somehow landed upright, sitting on its wheels, ready to drive on. I secretly worried that I just couldn't do this anymore, that my nerve would be too shaky, my skills inadequate. What if my courage failed me, or my balance, or my timing? I knew Eagle Rock was waiting just around the bend, and surely there would be many more difficult challenges. But facing upstream and using a front ferry this time, we made it through the haystacks just fine, and over to the other side. Everyone was relieved to see that our repaired canoe held, and performed well. I was encouraged to feel my skills re-surface quickly. They say that what doesn't kill you makes you stronger. That's probably true, but I certainly didn't feel stronger yet: just relieved to be alive, to still have a boat, and to be able to get out on the water again.

Otto and Kevin carefully hiked their gear down along river-right to their canoe, while the rest of us slowly lined our loaded boats, and safely floated them downriver, hugging the edge. Like cowboys guiding our black horses from shore with yellow ropes, we gradually got around the next few bends in the small canyon. After half an hour we joined Otto and Kevin, across from the cliff where they had stopped after almost swamping. Their canoe was waiting undisturbed, stowed upside-down, and tied to a tree just up from the shore. They untied the rope flipped their boat upright, carried it to the water's edge and loaded. Then on this much calmer, happier day, the group celebrated with a snack. We were ready to go on.

Looking directly across to the other side of this tight bend in the river, we could see a large eagle's nest perched under a rock overhang, two-thirds of the way up the sheer cliff. It was more than a metre across, and made of thick sticks that were as long as my arm. There was no eagle around, perhaps because we were there. But we were pretty sure that this was the home of the same wonderful golden eagle that had flown over us at Eagle Rock the day before, just as our pinned boat came free. When it left us to fly downriver, it had probably come here. And this bird, or its ancestors or its children, had likely been the source of our group's wonderful gift of feathers. This reminded me: everything is connected.

The Algonquin language has a special word to describe this: "Ginawaydaganuc." It holds a prayer: we are all connected; we are all related; everything is connected; everything is related. The word captures these beliefs and more: Ginawaydaganuc. With respect and caution, we pushed off. I took my customary last look back upstream, to the places gone by, and started paddling.

The river broadened gradually to over twenty metres, but it remained roller-coaster fast, with lots of quick bends and gravel bars. We would run a stretch, get out and scout, run the boats around six or seven more corners, do high speed shore eddy-outs to collect together, then scout some more. Everyone scanned as we went, looking for any debris from our boat.

At lunch we found the spare aluminum Mohawk paddle that the outfitter had given Roger, plus, inexplicably, my small roll of yellow duct tape that I had used along with a red roll as identification marks on the upper shafts of my two paddles near their handle grips. But that was all. These two items had somehow been deposited almost side by side. Near them, on the same gravel bar, were several full-sized upended willows, and some green spindly spruce trees that had obviously been recently washed away. There was evidence everywhere of extreme high water. It sank in further that we had been attempting to run Eagle Rock Canyon, in not just a heavy downpour, but during a major flood.

None of our other lost gear, including my beautiful wooden Grey Owl paddle, was found, at least not by our group. However, while searching for debris Roger did find a different kind treasure. Lying on one of the gravel bars that we got out on to search was a huge, broad moose horn or antler, with six points, or fingers. He picked it up and carefully laid it across the gear in our boat. It almost spanned the canoe. We would bring it home with us.

Around 1:00 p.m. the remaining clouds parted and we had full sun for what seemed like the first time in ages! Covering several more kilometres after lunch, we got tired from all of the cranking and pushing with our paddles, but it was an awesome feeling to be flying along the river again through incredible scenery. Although our paddling was mainly steering, it was impossible to know what might be coming up next, so we couldn't lose our focus for a second. We dodged many big rocks, and fallen, semi-floating spruce trees, that were often sticking out from shore into the river, and acting as sweepers.

Around 6:00 we came to the confluence of Black Feather Creek with the Mountain River. It was hard to believe, that only now were we beginning our journey on the actual Mountain. As our large tributary flowed in from river-right the Mountain River's size doubled. We stopped and looked around at the fabulous panoramic views. No longer closed in by canyons and steep mountainsides, we were now out in the flat open centre of an enormous natural bowl, with huge multi-coloured mountains surrounding us in the distance. We even had completely blue skies and blazing warm sunshine! We would be on the Mountain River from here on, and in every way it was glorious!

After ten more minutes the group pulled over at a great camping spot on river-left, close to the point where a small, crystal clear tributary flowed in. How wonderful it was to just relax and bake in the sun, with a sound boat, and no dam to build! For the first half hour, most of us simply lay prostrate on the pebbly gravel bar shore, soaking up the rays. Then we set up camp.

As of today we've been out a full week. What a week! Under the clear blue sky I took a solo walk after dinner and built Jill a small rock Inuksuk beside the edge of the little tributary. I miss her so much, and Jody, and Daniel, and Patrick.

———•◆•———

9

Along the way there were countless gifts: the
visions of every day, the air, the water, the earth,
the fire.

———•————

The early morning sky was pastel purple above the sweeping valley. It wasn't surprising that our guide friends had
labelled this spot "The Golf Course." No doubt a golfer would
be tempted to whack a few. The flat bottom of this mountain-
rimmed bowl is over one kilometre wide, and many kilometres
long. It's obvious that in the distant past this vast area has
been under deep water: the floor of a giant lake or some much
more immense Mountain River. Now mainly dry, except for
the present river and a few small creeks, this floodplain land is
made almost entirely of billions of deposited pebbles and small
rocks. On this July day it was dotted with colourful clumps of
delicate pink pea flowers, short-stalked fireweed, and our little
tents.

The Black Feather Creek water had been grey and gritty
for days, full of silt from the runoff caused by all the rain. The

Mountain River now flowing past our camp was the same colour. But fortunately the little nameless tributary creek pouring into it from our side was silt-free and beautifully clear. This delicious drinking water was a fabulous treat, the best since the Push-Pull headwaters. Last evening we had all filled our water bottles. I collected a big potful for morning coffee.

As we got close to breakfast time, thick clouds with darker shades of purple and grey came across the sky, dramatically dimming our light. Although we saw it coming from a long way off, we didn't move quickly enough, and barely had time to pack our personal stuff, take down the tents, and set up the big blue and white tarp and a second adjoining orange plastic tarp, before the rain poured down heavily on us at 8:00 a.m.

Roger and I were the day's cooks. We set up our breakfast fire in the trusty environmental stove, just under the edge of the tarp, and made excellent scrambled eggs from a mix. To make it extra tasty we added lots of real bacon. After feasting we all talked and laughed most of the morning away, as we again watched the rain spill off the tarp in hypnotic, twirling lines. Fortunately, by noon the rain had stopped, although the clouds remained. We packed up the tarps and the kitchen, loaded our canoes and launched.

Zooming off, we were exhilarated to be riding the wide Mountain River, and sped along for hours through the Golf Course valley. The river descended steadily as we floated along like logs on a high speed flume ride. Very little paddling was needed, yet we flew at our fastest speed so far. The moving water even seemed to create its own wind, helping us along. I mainly rode rudder, while Roger did an occasional draw or pry stroke, pulling us slightly to one side, or pushing to the other. Even when coasting, we flew past the shoreline faster than a quick runner could run. The pitch was so steep that several times it felt as if we were on a massive escalator – falling down the river.

The valley opened wider as the river floated our canoes past magnificent mountains of blue, purple, grey, orange, silver and gold. Overwhelmed by beauty and scale, I wished I could somehow capture these visions in a painting, but then thought to myself that to paint any of these vistas would require not only an extremely talented artist with a full palette of pigments, but also the largest possible canvas. Nature was the creator here, freely giving incredible, dreamlike visions everywhere we looked. There were no signs of the work of human hands anywhere, except on our paddles.

Although we were given a wonderful easy ride by the current, everyone had to stay alert, watching for shoals, gravel bars, side currents, rocks, and wrong turns down dead end channels. Sometime these would quickly drain off and become drier shallow fans, or simply run out of enough water to be able to float a boat. We would occasionally have to step out for a minute or two, in a few centimetre of trickling water, and haul our canoes back up the channel a short way, to take a different, deeper fork.

The signature features of the river are undeniably its many braided channels. On Black Feather Creek we had experienced a few braids, especially as we approached the junction with the Mountain, but now they were more frequent and on a grander scale. We found our topographical maps gave only an approximation of where the main channels might be on any given day, since most of the gravel bars shifted constantly, depending on the changing water levels, weather and season. The eagle eyes in our lead boat brought us the right way almost every time.

At 4:00 we arrived at a second icefield, this one only on river-left. We pulled over and hopped out. The compacted snow and ice was again white on top, and along its open river side it was the deep turquoise colour of a glacier. At four metres tall, this icefield was slightly higher than the one on Black Feather Creek. The mouths of a few smooth, oval caves opened outwards towards the river. One of these hollows was even big enough that we could hop inside, two at a time, and pose reclining for photos. Daniel and Jody would love it!

Playing a little helped us all relax. We joked, ate snacks, and looked over the maps. The group mood was still somewhat tense, after the huge stresses at Eagle Rock. Now and then there was a sharp word, or a hint of brittleness to a conversation. As often happens, it's the time after a crisis has passed, when people's emotions process the real dangers of what happened, and of what could have happened. Successfully paddling great whitewater in the wilderness for the last two days had boosted our spirits and exorcised most of our residual fears and frustrations. Now, thanks to a little play, we all felt better.

Odile is kindly letting me share her camera, since mine is lost. I'm at least able to give her rolls of print film, because I have several that were safely buried in my pack during the wreck. Like Kevin's gift of a new journal, which has allowed me to write again, being able to take a few of my own photographs helps me feel less shaky, more whole, more back to normal. She's such a positive, thoughtful person, always giving everyone kind words, and trying to help. I think she knows I'm still feeling pretty wounded, still trying to heal.

Our professional cameramen, Roger and Kevin, are also shooting away, mainly slides, and sometimes with the video camera. The rig that we have allows us to recharge the video battery via solar cells, except so far, because of all of the rain and cloud on so many of our days, it has often been impossible to charge it. But today it was working.

Wave after wave of clouds and their undulating blue and purple shadows washed across us all afternoon as we flew along, but the rain held off. Although we didn't start paddling until noon, we still traveled 27 kilometres, our best distance so far. All of us are tired and achy, but we feel great because we've made such excellent progress, and it's been so beautiful. Even though we've been mainly steering, it's been a workout. However, once, for ten minutes the river calmed enough to allow us all to raft up. Holding on to each other's gunwales, our four boats sailed along the wide river together, a pleasant first.

We set up camp on a large, dry, gravel delta on river-left. It was created long-ago by the extended outwash of what we could see was once a large tributary washing down from Shale Lake. The weather has remained pleasant all evening, and the sky seems to promise clearing. We saw grizzly bear tracks and wolf tracks close to camp, but no-one worried much that our noisy group, with our bear-proof plastic food barrels, would get a visitor. It was just nice to know they were around. We were the visitors.

Cooking again meant very little down time for Roger and I. While doing our chores we joked back and forth about the two of us doing all the work. Thankfully this sort of good-natured banter has returned.

Brian tried his luck at fishing but had no nibbles. The cloudy, grey water, loaded with silt, means that his lure disappears from view after sinking just a few centimetres. Any fish probably wouldn't be able to see it. But he had a very pleasant time anyway, relaxing, enjoying the view, and looking very much the iconic wilderness fisherman.

After another late evening wander, where I again enjoyed the abundant pink fireweed and incredible 360° mountain vistas, I retired to my tent at 11:00, and worked on drying off the insides of my little binoculars. Their lenses had become fogged by condensation and rain. I was amazed to be able to do this kind of work, and also to write in my journal, until well after midnight, without any need of a flashlight. I've been wearing my touque to bed most nights, sometimes pulling it down over my eyes, just to get a semblance of real darkness. We don't see much midnight sun though, or mid-day sun either.

———•—•———

10

We almost died. Can this be seen as a gift? Yes, I think so, because of the "almost" part. To some extent I felt invincible before this trip, but I came back much more humble, vulnerable, mortal. I was given insight. I know that endings can indeed happen, and caution must be ever-present. I also learned to not give up.

———•—————

I woke with a start, thinking, "Damn! Rain again!" Since our camp was on a low gravel delta by the mouth of a tributary, my immediate next thought was of a possible repeat flash flood. Mercifully there would be none on this day but, as an extra precaution, after scrambling to pack my own gear and crawling out of the tent, I rushed around moving the big blue and white tarp and all our kitchen stuff to higher ground.

As we ate breakfast underneath, with those little curling waterfalls again dribbling off the corners, everyone chatted and joked, trying to raise spirits. But our bravado is wearing thin. Everyone has become so discouraged by the weather.

When the downpour eased to a drizzle in the late morning, we broke camp, loaded and paddled on, hoping it would eventually clear. Fortunately we didn't experience any driving rain or thunder, but the wet stuff continued for most of the day. Everyone did great paddling as we booted along, travelling an incredible 49 kilometres, almost double yesterday's distance.

In a few welcome quiet stretches, when the rain let up and we whipped along just steering, Roger and I could hear a faint "clickity, clickity, clack" rattling sound coming from somewhere deep beneath our canoe. This lovely musical sound resembled that of a cactus rain stick, or little clicking wooden wind chimes in a gentle breeze. Eventually we realized it was being produced by countless small pebbles and rocks, probably the same types we saw deposited on every gravel bar by the river, as they rolled, bumped and bounced their way along the riverbed, propelled by the strong current. Somewhere down there, each one of them was clickity clacking their way towards the Mackenzie. We too were being moved along by the same waters. The comforting little sounds reminded me that a river is constantly and forever changing, and so are we.

Now and then we would pull over, get out, stretch, have a snack, drink some water, look over the maps, share a few laughs, then hop back in and ride some more. During a couple of these stops the group took longer breaks, and went for short hikes. On one of them we went to see "The Fountain of Youth," which was a very unusual dribbling hillside, made of nature's geyserites, algae and precipitate. I thought of Jody's high school experiments, and picked up a few small rock samples for her.

God, I miss you all. Last night I again took out all my photos and stared at everyone for 20 minutes. This is such a fabulous trip, but I'll be glad to be home.

We didn't roll into camp tonight until 8:00, but are now set up on the four metre high bank of a major tributary called Cache Creek. Our tents are on the river-left shore, a few hundred metres up from its confluence with the Mountain River. Again the label "Creek" is quite inaccurate. This high volume waterway is at least a hundred metres wide. Back home it would certainly be called a river, a big river.

On its far shore, the much higher and steeper banks form the base of a tall mountain. The waterway itself seems to be located on an old fault line. During some former era, the entire far side for many kilometres must have been heaved skyward a full kilometre to form the present mountains. We've camped on the more open floodplain side, where the terraced shoreline indicates several water level fluctuations, both recent and in the distant past. As with the Golf Course, many thousands of years ago this location was surely the bottom of a vast body of water, rimmed by the tops of mountains.

Today's river, with its spacious wide flats of mud and gravel, is a safe four metres below the level of our camp, but it can be reached quickly via a steep walk down an opening in the gravel cliff. Besides all of our gear, we also hauled our canoes up that opening and tied them to bushes right beside camp, just in case. To maximize our dry zone in the continuing wet, we set up our orange plastic tarp adjacent to the big blue and white nylon one.

It's an easy ten minute stroll down along the flats to a spectacular vantage point near where Cache Creek flows into the Mountain River. We can look a few hundred metres directly across the combined waters, and stare right into the tall, open mouth of First Canyon. The Mountain River's canyons are numbered by how one approaches them from the headwaters when going downstream towards the Mackenzie. This being the first big canyon on the main river, it is called First Canyon. The gaping entrance looks awesome and intimidating.

The next time we break camp, we will have to immediately paddle into that canyon. There's only one way in, one way through. Backing up will be impossible. High cliffs stand sentinel on either side, towering 30 to 50 metres above the narrow 15 metre wide channel of deep, fast water. If troubles arise, there will be no refuge on those sheer walls. Any attempted portage, to try to bypass this tight river gate, would require a long, dangerous hike up and along the steep, wet mountainsides. No, we will have to paddle right into that scary opening – but not tonight.

The group will rest up, while waiting for better weather. No-one wants more problems. Our individual and group confidence is still a little shaky. The water level continues to be abnormally high and the rain just seems to go on and on. I hope the sun comes out soon, and stays out! Everything is saturated and dripping.

In camp we are all quiet and pensive. After an evening feast of pemmican and a dehydrated veggie mix, I've withdrawn to write in our tent, where it is warmer and drier. It's good to lie down. I smile as I think of those billions of pebbles, each clickity, clickity, clacking their way down the river. We all roll along.

11

I was given wanderlust dreams, which, in many ways, have gone on to my children. Who knows where they will go, and what they will pass along to others.

———————

Today was our second no-travel day of the trip. We were supposed to hike around the area, and maybe try to climb the far shore mountain to scout the big canyon from above. But everyone just stayed in bed late because it was so dank, cool, and dim. It continued to rain throughout the night, and was still drizzling at 9:00 a.m. so I rolled over and slept in. At 12:45 I heard the call that breakfast coffee was ready, and so crawled out, even though the air was still full of mist.

At 2:00 the rain stopped, and at 4:00 the sun came out for one beautiful hour. But the clouds moved back in, and at 6:30 it rained on us hard again. Finally, about 9:00 p.m. it stopped again, but the sky stayed overcast. A chilly wind came up and the temperature dropped further. By 10:00 p.m. it was only 11°C. Now, at 11:00, it seems as if the sky is trying to clear, so maybe tomorrow will be better. Looking over this journal I see that I'm mentioning the weather quite a bit. It is having a profound effect on us all.

Despite the weather, we took a few short exploratory hikes in our rain gear during the afternoon and evening. On one solo walk, after heading down towards the confluence, I sat near the top of a spruce ridge by a small, trickling waterfall with interesting calcium deposits and algae. For the first time since our layover day on Black Feather Creek, I had dug out my art supplies. Sitting in that beautiful spot I drew a charcoal and conté sketch of the downriver view, featuring the big, waiting mouth of First Canyon.

Afterwards a group of us hiked roughly half a kilometre upstream to another, larger waterfall that flowed into Cache Creek. I picked up a few more keeper rocks for Jody, including a purple one which was cut into several clean slices like salami. We climbed up and around the waterfall, exploring large pieces of the conglomerate rock strewn about like chunks of rough cement with rocks embedded in them, and found more algae and calcium deposits. Near the top of the little falling stream was a natural stone bridge, 5 x 2 m, made completely out of a thin shelf of conglomerate rock. It spanned a pool of clear water. The ground water trickled from some unseen source through the rocks above the bridge, spilled across it lengthwise like a viaduct, then poured off both sides in graceful transparent veils into the pool. No artist could have designed a more beautiful sculpture. We crawled under the bridge, taking pictures looking out through the veils. I thought to myself, if the temperature was warmer, this would be an idyllic place to swim. I also thought that this whole Cache Creek area is the type of extraordinary place where epic myths might be written or set.

Each day I find I am feeling more directly tuned in to nature, with an intensity and purity I've never felt before. It's a wonderful kind of high. For the last couple of days I've had to suppress the strong urge to bring home a whole boatful of the gorgeous river stones. Every flower is a starburst, a delicate sculpture, a beautiful photograph to frame. The woodsmoke smell on my hands and clothes is a comfort. The majesty and complexities of the mountains seem to increase all the time, like respect for a friend, as one comes to know them.

I've heard it said, albeit usually by people who aren't trippers, that on a journey like this, a certain type of personal sensory deprivation happens, caused by the simplification of life and a reduction of stimulus input. But I know that, at least for me, the opposite is true. The more time I spend in the wild, the more my understanding opens to the wonders, beauty, and indescribable complexities all around. Rather than decreasing, my stimulus input deepens, without the myriad distractions that clutter city life. My life outdoors is richer. I see little nuances of colours on the mountainsides, savour each ingredient of meals, and smell the difference between wet trees and dry ones. I listen to small birds call from a long way off, and hear others answer back nearby, and try to think of what they might be saying. I hear my own breathing, the cycle of inward and outward, and can sometimes also imagine that I hear other quiet whispers, voices in the wind, and in the waters. These are not hallucinatory, but rather come from the intimate connection with the land, water and sky, and from taking the time to be open to the natural world. I feel as if neglected parts of my brain are being engaged. I think more clearly, often about profound things, such as who am I in this vast world, or the simple beauty of a boat that floats. It is such good medicine to be here: even with all the rain; even with all our difficulties. My spirit is boosted. My heart is stronger.

It has been restorative, having this relaxing camp day. Tensions have eased further. But we all know there is a huge challenge coming up tomorrow. Weather permitting, we will paddle into the canyon first thing. It looks daunting: a long, dangerous run. We are excited and looking forward to an incredible experience, but we're also worried.

Somewhere around camp today Brian lost his big eagle feather. He doesn't know how. It was in his hat yesterday, but though he had secured it quite well, it somehow came loose. If it's true that these things come to you when the time is right, why had it suddenly left him now? He, Kevin and Roger spent a couple of hours thoroughly searching the whole area, but it was never found.

As I lay in our tent waiting for drowsiness, I looked over the maps again, and made some notes:

- By the end of our trip, our overall distance travelled from Willow Handle Lake to the mouth of the Mountain River at the Mackenzie River will be 302 kilometres.
- Day 1 we flew in to Willow Handle.
- Day 2 we travelled 11 kilometres – from Willow Handle Lake to our layover camp of two nights, just past the ice-field on Black Feather Creek.
- Because of the layover on Day 3, the Eagle Rock wreck on Day 4, and the following two days of dam building and recovery, by the end of Day 7 we had only gone a further 14 kilometres.
- This gave us a total of 25 kilometres from our start on Willow Handle to the Golf Course camp near the confluence of Black Feather Creek and the Mountain River.

- On Day 8 we left the Golf Course, paddling to our gravel delta camp, where the tributary came in from Shale Lake, travelling 27 kilometres.
- Then yesterday, Day 9, we did our biggest distance so far, paddling 49 kilometres from the Shale Lake tributary delta camp to our current location, here beside Cache Creek.
- So, in our 10 days on-the-river, we have travelled 101 kilometres, or one third of our total distance, and have come from Willow Handle Lake to Cache Creek.
- This leaves us 201 kilometres still to go in 7 days, including five canyons.

I left my calculations to go back to focussing on the incredible here and now, remembering that it is not the destination that is the most important, but the trip itself. We would only sleep this one last night here at Cache Creek. I thought over all we had seen.

Pulling on my touque for the night I lay back in my sleeping bag and looked with unfocussed eyes at the roof of the tent, feeling very much alive. Breathing slowly in and out, savouring the air, I listened to the marvellous, distant sound of whitewater in the night. It was rumbling, singing, whispering. During a lull in the wind, I shut my eyes and drifted off.

12

How can adversity be understood as a gift? Yet it is. Adversity that is endured, or better yet overcome, gives courage, understanding, strength, faith, healing, determination, and sometimes the wisdom to prevent mistakes from happening again.

There are so many metaphors that refer to this: the metal being tested in the fire and made stronger; the ship weathering the gale and making it to new worlds; the struggling soldiers who at last succeed; the crop which survives floods, droughts, winds and disease, and is harvested with seeds to grow anew; the person who endures a long quest and at last sees their vision; the very old woman or man who, in the end, is able to tell their grandchildren some of the best things they've learned.

Mouth of First Canyon, Mountain River, from the shore of Cache Creek, which is coming in from the right.

– charcoal and conté sketch, Phil Weir

I smiled to think that even in heaven it rains. How else would the rivers run? The weather had improved to cloudy with a few sunny breaks as we loaded cheerfully, our adrenalin running high. Like those clickity, clacking pebbles, we were continuing on. I wondered if I might be back someday. A beautiful song came to mind, written by master singer-songwriter Michael Peter Smith, from Chicago. It's called "Colleen's Song." Part of the lyrics say:

Some day...
In the rain...
In the sun...
I will see you again…
Some day...
Some time...
Or never....

...We are here for a moment, then gone…to sometime…or never.

Shortly after leaving our Eagle Rock camp, Roger and I had started calling our canoe the "Mary Ellen Carter the Second." She had performed really well so far, but was about to be put to a major test. Remembering the huge difference made to our safety back there, when fast water had instantly flooded the canoe after we touched the rock, Roger and I had taken the extra precaution of covering our bow with a makeshift spray cover. We improvised, using part of a roll of thick drop-sheet plastic which had been brought along in the group gear. Using lots of duct tape, we had secured it to the front of our boat, hoping it might give the little section in front of Roger a bit of increased protection in the big stuff we knew was coming right up.

Chatting yesterday, both of us had convinced ourselves that if we had only brought professional heavy duty boat-length spray covers (also called spray decks or spray skirts) on the trip, and had them on, tightly covering the boat when we first bumped into Eagle Rock, then probably the water would have been held back a bit, and would have just poured off – at least at first. That way, maybe our boat wouldn't have been flooded, and rolled so quickly. We further reasoned that this would have given us the few moments needed to finish manoeuvring slightly further to the right. Then we could have edged safely past Eagle Rock. In short, we reasoned, with the crystal clarity and bravado of hindsight, that with a full expedition-quality spray deck on our canoe, our wreck wouldn't have happened at all.

At least that was our theory, perhaps our fantasy. Still, we had no proper spray cover to help us now, so we created a make-shift partial one. Maybe it might give us an extra moment or two at some critical time. The others declined for now.

Our second theory about the dump was that, since a back ferry takes a little time to set up and execute, at least for us, and since we weren't very experienced at doing a lot of them in big current, then perhaps we shouldn't have continued trying to stick with that particular manoeuvre in the last few seconds we had left before hitting the rock. Maybe, when it became likely that our strong back paddling for the back ferry wasn't going to get us past the side of that rock fast enough, we should have made a sudden switch and done a few strong forward power and steering strokes instead. This, we calmly reasoned, could have pushed us quickly hard to the right, and clear of the obstacle. So, although the back ferry remained our first choice manoeuvre for moving laterally while facing downriver, and we vowed to improve our skills at executing it, we also made a mental note: sometimes, if the back ferry couldn't be set up in time, powering hard forward towards the destination side might be a better option. Experience would tell.

After a couple of nights' rest everyone was cautiously ready to face the canyon. Its ominous gate waited, with those giant cliffs, deep shadows, and an immediate blind curve to the right. We knew the opening was just the beginning of this long canyon's run, but, due to the wet weather and slippery conditions on the steep mountainside, we hadn't been able to scout it from above as we had hoped. Without direct scouting, we knew we were light on information, and planned to stop to gather more along the way, when conditions allowed. Our notes from home, maps and strategy discussions would help, but we knew it would be our wits and skills, combined with the river's good grace, that would be needed to see us safely through.

Pushing off from the campsite, we hugged the left shore of Cache Creek and slowly paddled five minutes down to the confluence. The Mountain River was barrelling past from left to right, at a higher speed than the inflow of the so-called creek. We were back at our turning point, where two days ago we had turned right and travelled upstream to camp. This time we turned our canoes left, and paddled back up along the river-right shore of the Mountain River a few metres, against its oncoming current, until we reached the bottom end of a shore gravel bar. There, at a point less than half a kilometre from the canyon's mouth, we beached our boats, stepped out on the stones, and peered with our binoculars into the gap.

The sedimentary rock layers on the left-side cliffs at the entrance were all tilted on a 45° diagonal pattern, with lines going roughly upwards, and to the right. They gave the impression that the cliff was leaning downstream, as if the strata had started off perpendicular to the earth, then somehow the river had pushed the rock to lean in its direction. The right wall was in deep shadow, but we guessed that the rock strata there probably had the same sort of tilted pattern, leaning downstream. The river made a slight bend to the right, just inside the mouth, then disappeared from view behind the entrance cliff. That was all we could see.

These huge mountains, which had been thrust up so high in the distant past, had also at some time apparently cracked right to their core, creating this single, narrow chasm, the only opening for the entire Mountain River to flow into. We studied our topographical maps one last time. The area coming up immediately after the entrance was hard to read, having so many elevation lines jammed together.

As always we left several boat-lengths between canoes. Otto and Kevin led off, while Roger and I tensely watched, at the ready, sitting in our boat. I tugged my hat brim down a bit, and checked to make sure I had my chinstrap on. The others remained on shore for the moment, standing by their canoes. They would hop in and follow as soon as we started. Quickly the lead canoe disappeared from view behind the first cliff. It was our turn.

Focussing on every stroke, Roger and I approached as slowly as the current allowed. Then with great care we floated around the first bend, and down into the hidden insides of the mouth. Otto and Kevin were already out of sight.

The current picked up speed, and the cliffs rose even higher, soon towering above us 80 metres, straight up on both sides. Our maps had shown that, somewhere up high, these walls bent away from the water slightly, then continued climbing steeply, ultimately rising a further 700 metres to the summits. From our tiny boat, deep in the bottom of the huge canyon, we didn't have a line of sight all the way to the mountain tops. But we could certainly see the massive cliffs closing in tighter, and feel the strong, swirling currents quickly begin to buffet us harder.

Almost immediately we were barrelling down a 100 metre straightaway. Surging water shook the boat, as we were flanked by haystack rollers and heaving swells of rising water – boils! This was the biggest, most intimidating water I had ever paddled, and we were inside the grandest scale rock cathedral I had ever been in. At the bottom of the first long chute was a blind tight bend to the left. Roger and I braced on either side of the boat and steered the best we could, trying to keep it level, as our canoe flew around the corner. We took in water, but we made it.

Once around, we could see Otto and Kevin a little further down, pulled over beside the left wall, facing us. They had managed to get close to the cliff, rotate in the deep fast water, and pull alongside. We steered towards them, eddied out of the main current just behind their boat, and backed up to cling with our fingertips to a small nook in the sheer rock. It was hard to gauge the depth of the rushing water but it was obviously quite deep. The cliffs continued going way down into the black. As we tried to stay stationary for a few moments, Roger and I rapidly bailed. My feet and knees were already in a few centimetres of ice water. Then the four of us peeled back into the main current, our boat a few seconds after theirs, and we zoomed down around two more bends.

The vertical rock walls now rose an incredible 90 metres on either side, and still descended straight down into the dark water. Otto and Kevin were able to get over to the side a second time, rotate their boat to aim upriver, and sit clinging with their fingers to a small notch in the cliff face. Roger and I tried to join them, but this time couldn't quite make it over to the wall. As we made our 180° turn and tried to pull alongside, the strong current stopped our progress and started to push our nose backwards. We knew that if we resisted we would quickly be propelled down the canyon in high-speed reverse. This was definitely not our preferred option, so we kept the canoe turning, and peeled right back into the main current, making it a donut, or a 360°. We sped on, suddenly becoming lead boat.

Working intensely to try to keep it steady and straight, we flew across the rollers and around the next blind bend to the left, remembering to hug the inside as much as possible. Once around, we saw that up ahead the cliff-top dropped down on the right to a low narrow ledge of rocky land at river level. To get there, we had to back ferry our boat quickly all the way across the river to river-right. Getting our angle, motion and tilt just right this time, we zoomed over in seconds. We then did a fast shore eddy-out, like cracking a whip, and both jumped onto shore. In the same fluid motion we pulled our Mary Ellen Carter the Second up onto the small lip of rock, and congratulated each other with high-fives.

But our joy was brief. Roger and I had now travelled roughly a kilometre and a half into the long canyon. We had barely finished securing our boat, and were standing holding our throwbags at the ready when, with a bolt of fear, we saw it. Low in the water, an upside-down black canoe came barrelling around the corner towards us! Someone had gone down! We could see no swimmers and no visible loose gear in the water. This probably meant everything was still tethered underneath. But where were the people? And which boat was it?

We blasted our whistles three times, over and over, while jogging a few steps along shore beside the runaway, to see if we might be able to hook a paddle or a throwbag line. It was no use. The belly-up canoe was too far out, right in the middle of the main current, flying along at top speed. Any line would have just floated off, with no-one to grab or tie it. We stared as it passed by. I briefly thought of jumping into our boat and chasing it; but no, the priority is always people. Make sure the people are safe first! Worry about boats and gear later. We had missing friends. They were probably in the water. Anxiously looking upriver for anyone floating towards us from around the bottom corner of the cliff, we could only glance behind as the black whaleback of the canoe rocketed away. After a slight bend to the left, it shot down the middle of a straightaway for half a kilometre. Then, chillingly, it sped around a blind corner to the right, and disappeared. It was gone! Still there were no people.

After a stunned silence, Roger and I found our legs and scrambled back up the narrow lip of shore as far as we could to the corner. Holding the base of the cliff and peering around, we were able to see upriver a little way. Stopped in their canoe, over at a very thin ledge of shore on the far side, were Pat and Brian, our sweep boat. So they were OK. We yelled back and forth but could barely hear them over the roar of the water and the echoing cliffs. We learned that it was Bert and Odile that had gone over. They had both made it safely to shore, thank God. Otto and Kevin were with them.

We later learned that Bert and Odile had capsized near the very beginning of the canyon, in those first big haystacks and boils. As we had witnessed, their canoe was upside-down, speeding downriver. Tied into it was all of their personal gear and some of the group gear, including the pots and the big nylon tarp. Once again our group was short a boat. And we still hadn't finished First Canyon!

Resisting repeated urges to tear after the runaway canoe, which would have been quite unsafe in the situation, Roger and I waited about fifteen minutes on shore until finally, both our lead and sweep boats paddled in together to join us on river-right. At least our three canoes and the six of us were back together.

Otto and Kevin told us that Odile and Bert were hiking up a notch in the canyon wall on river-left. From there they would hike along the top of the giant cliffs until they would hopefully find a point at the end of the canyon where they could climb down and meet up with us. It was their only way, since Otto and Kevin's boat was fully loaded with gear.

Getting back in our canoes we were extremely focussed as we began paddling the path of the lost boat. We soon went around the corner where it had vanished. The rushing river just continued on and disappeared again around the next bend. No boat.

Our information told us that shortly after the next curve to the left there would be a tricky sharp turn to the right. It most certainly looked that way as we approached. More sheer 80 metre cliffs closed in tightly on both sides, narrowing the flow. We knew we were about to confront a very difficult challenge. Just before a fast thin 'V' shaped funnel that would lead us to the bend, there was a small area on river-right where we were able go ashore and scout. It was a far from perfect viewing spot, just the jumbled talus base of an old rockslide. But we had to take a look before going on, and there was no other place. We stepped out, secured our boats, and scrambled up a few metres.

The scene ahead gave me the shivers. We stood huddled, still recovering from the first section of the canyon, and saw that we now faced a faster, narrower, and more dangerous stretch. The entire river picked up speed as it was further compressed by the cliffs, and blasted through a narrow gap of only eight metres. The rock strata lines still showed the same 45° diagonal pattern, going upwards and leaning downriver, that we had seen at the entrance. However this time there would be no chance of pulling over, no hanging on with fingertips. The current flew past the walls in tumultuous, splashing swirls and swells. To get close to either edge would almost certainly dump a canoe. Even more sobering, for as far as we could see, there was no potential rescue spot.

For a few minutes we were speechless, searching for a safe way through. There didn't seem to be one. The initial "V" of the main current quickly became a thin, waving line. To the right of centre the water boiled and heaved, as if in a giant kettle. To the left we counted three shifting whirlpools. Around the corner there were probably more. Everyone agreed that the way to go had to be along the very narrow tongue of fast current between the boils and whirlpools. In most cases this would be roughly down the middle, but making the run much harder, this wet tongue was not only wagging from side to side. It was also heaving up and down! No route stayed stable or predicable. Pushed by the continuously changing movements of boils and whirlpools, our path waited, thrashed, and roared!

Accepting that this fickle tongue was our only way through, we stared at the water for a few more minutes, thinking. We knew the risks. Everything was still very swollen from many days of rain. Dangerously high water had caused us major difficulties at Eagle Rock. We were already down one boat. Odile and Bert were hiking along the cliff tops somewhere on the far side, after experiencing frightening, dangerous swims. They were alone in an unknown landscape, their boat gone. The two of them had no gear, no map, and no food. They were counting on us.

Like most real-life gauntlets, there was just no way around it. We couldn't possibly portage this section by somehow hauling our canoes high up along the cliffs. Also, because of the strong current and the vertical walls, it was impossible to retreat back up the canyon. No, we would have to run it. In my pocket, I held the sweetgrass tightly.

Our scouting complete, we prepared for the run. The three boats were carefully lined back up the steep shore a few metres. There, a small gravel bar with deep fast water on the far side served as our launching point. Leaving a minute between canoes, each pair hopped in and rode it like a wild mustang. Otto and Kevin led off, and made it through skilfully. Anxiously watching from behind, Roger and I saw the river dramatically lift and lower their boat three times as they whipped along the twisting line. The surging water changed constantly.

Pulling our boat into the current to follow, Roger and I also managed to hit our initial target, the sweet spot on the heaving line. Bracing steadily, and riding three big lifts and lowers while winding right down the middle, we took in a couple of heavy splashes of water from our left near the start, but we were OK. Thank heavens for our new mini spray-skirt!

A little further down, after the bend, the canyon opened a bit. Otto and Kevin were able to do a quick eddy turn along the left cliff. They pulled in next to the wall, and inched back into a deep crevice. Sheltered from the main current, they sat and waited. This time we managed to do the same manoeuvre and joined them. As Roger and I again quickly bailed a few centimetres of water, everyone anxiously watched and waited. Our last boat was overdue.

It felt like ten minutes before Pat and Brian finally came around that corner. As each moment ticked by, we knew the delay was definitely not good. We prepared ourselves, with throwbags and paddles at the ready. When their canoe did finally speed into view, it was riding incredibly low, almost completely full of water. With only a couple of centimetres of freeboard left to keep them afloat, they were obviously in critical condition. Riding fast, with paddles bracing on both sides, and looks of intense concentration and anguish on both faces, they flew past us, locked in the middle of the main current. Too full and heavy to be able to manoeuvre at all, and desperately trying to hold their boat steady, they were about to go under.

Otto and Kevin immediately peeled into the main current to help, but couldn't reach them in time. Like a runaway train, there was no stopping or steering that high-speed canoe full of water. We could only watch as within seconds of passing us, Pat and Brian's boat lumbered hard sideways to the right, then rolled completely over. Our friends spilled into the fast, frigid water, suddenly swimming for their lives. Even if we could catch them, there was no sign ahead of a lowering in the vertical walls, no safe place to get to shore. This canyon still had a long way to go.

They swam along just behind their capsized boat: Brian first, then Pat a couple of metres back, both of them caught in the centre of the deepest, strongest current. Their heads were up, but each was sucked under a few times in turbulence and small whirlpools. Both rescue canoes tried to reach them with throwbags, but it was no use. Racing close behind, Otto, Kevin, Roger and I pumped flat out, but were only able to gain on them slightly. While paddling our strongest in full rescue mode, we also had to keep focused and make sure that we maintained our own stability. A crucial safety rule for rescuers is: "Don't make a bad situation worse!" With two out of four boats now down, it was crucial that we keep our heads and not lose another one.

For 200 metres the canyon remained narrow as our line of belly-up boat, swimmers, and chase canoes whipped around three more bends. Increasingly frustrated and frightened, and imagining the terror of our friends, we paddled as hard as we dared, but weren't able to out-muscle the current and catch them. We knew how cold that water was, and what it would be quickly doing to them. Brian's head went under a couple more times up ahead. Time was running out. It was imperative we get them out of there before the unthinkable happened.

Otto and Kevin stayed with Brian. Their canoe was also closer to the capsized boat than ours, so Roger and I concentrated on Pat, who was now floating slightly further back. Fortunately he had the presence of mind and ability to keep hold of his paddle. This was helping him steer a bit with his arms, as he floated rapidly along, face forward, with his feet up in front of him, in the recommended "safety" or "go-cart" position. At one point he was again briefly sucked down part way into a whirlpool, but managed to break free and popped back up, paddle still in hand.

Finally, after five minutes, with Pat about eight metres ahead of our canoe, the canyon walls lowered slightly and the river valley opened wide. Gravel beaches and low islands now lined both sides. At this point, roughly a kilometre from where they had capsized, Pat was finally able to make it over to the left shore and self-rescue at a section where the canyon's wall was edged by a low pebble beach. Exhausted, barely conscious, and hypothermic, he crawled out, lay down by the water's edge, and closed his eyes.

In seconds Roger and I had blasted our way to shore right beside him, finally catching up. We used a snap shore eddy-out, beached the boat, and ran to assist. In less than two minutes from when he touched land we were crouched by his side, immediately giving First Aid for hypothermia. We put our warm hands on his cold skin, began to warm him, talked with him, encouraged him, tried to get him to open his eyes, tried to reassure and comfort him. But he was in very rough shape.

Meanwhile we knew another man's life was also still in danger. As we worked with Pat we glanced across the river, which was by now over 200 metres wide. Half a kilometre down on the shore of a large gravel bar island, we could see that Otto and Kevin's boat was beached beside what looked like the capsized canoe. As we watched, we saw Brian stagger out of the water, with Kevin near him. Thank God he was OK.

But our urgent, pressing concern was Pat, who was in critical condition. Although out of the frigid water, he was still in great danger. We kept working, but his face was growing paler. His lips were grey, his breathing getting shallower. He couldn't talk. Only semi-conscious, he occasionally moaned softly, incoherently. Even with us holding him, talking to him, trying to warm him, his skin remained cold. Pat was wearing his full wetsuit, which had surely helped, and Roger had put his own PFD over top of Pat's legs to help warm him, but the long frigid swim, exhaustion, and fear had taken their toll. The best we could get from him were a few garbled mumbles. He was also not shivering: a sure sign of danger. We continued First Aid for hypothermia and shock, and became increasingly concerned about his heart.

In the triage of crisis management, I wouldn't allow myself to think for more than a moment about my deepest unspoken fear. But it weighed on me like a cold stone. He might die right then and there. Oh my God, how could we let this happen to our friend? We had to help him. I forced myself to draw on every reserve of courage and First Aid knowledge, every trick of warming, coaching, caring, of tenacity, of giving hope.

These poured out of me in a blur in those few minutes, but fear weighed increasingly on us as we saw little progress, and a gradual lessening of Pat's consciousness.

Who knows what it is in the end that makes the difference during a time like this? Some things are within our control and some things simply aren't. We all just did our best.

At that moment two very fortuitous things happened. They were almost unbelievably opportune and suddenly helped turn the tide. Odile and Bert, who since their spill had been hiking along the top of the high cliffs on our side of the river, just happened to be at a point above us, on the cliffs over the gravel beach, where they could look down and see the crisis situation. This was our first huge piece of luck.

The second was that, at that precise location, just above the gravel beach where we were working with Pat, there also happened to be a deep cleft in the high cliff wall. This small gully enabled Bert and Odile to be able to safely climb down to where we were, and help. There hadn't been a single other safe place like this, where they could get access to the water's edge, for the entire length of the long canyon, their hike of about four kilometres so far. By some grace, there it was, exactly where and when it was needed most. Bert and Odile had completed their own arduous journey, high along the top of the canyon, and they now came down to help us. What a fabulous surprise it was for Roger and I, as we knelt beside Pat, to look up and see them rush over to assist. Once again my heart was warmed with the knowledge that the support of friends is never more welcome than when the going is toughest.

Now we were five together again on river-left. We all worked to reassure Pat, talking to him, continuing to warm him, placing our six warm hands and arms on his cold hands, face and neck. With one of us under each arm, half-carrying him as he staggered, we got him back from the water's edge to a safer, more sheltered spot at the base of the cliff. A big bonfire was quickly lit and we began gradually warming him thoroughly. Slowly, Pat struggled his way back.

At first he needed to be propped up, in order to be able to sit by the fire against the cliff wall without slumping sideways. After a little while he was able to squat with support, but it took fifteen more minutes before he could stand on his own. Even then, he was weak and had to be helped to walk, though he was soon able to speak slowly. We all sat back down with him by the fire's warmth, and after another half hour he could get up and walk well without assistance. As he continued to recover, we stayed close beside him, ready to deal with any setback. An hour after making it to shore he was doing well.

But he was understandably shaken. He'd had the stuffing knocked out of him. Although he had rallied successfully, each of us, and most especially Pat, knew that he had come far too close to death. A scare like that is the kind of experience you never forget: a terribly close call, followed by a very special second chance. Working as a group and given Pat's ability to recover, the gifts of luck, grace, providence and the river had all gotten him through this very rough time. Thank God.

At the same time, on the opposite shore another drama was unfolding. From later discussions we learned that Kevin and Otto had finally caught Brian in the canyon just as he was being swirled around the edge of a large whirlpool. Before they could get close to him his head went under twice. Desperate to help, in a split-second flash of dread Kevin had wondered what on earth he would tell their mother! But thank goodness

Brian's head bobbed back up again and they were able to get their canoe right beside him without being drawn into the twirling water. Brian reached up and grabbed the gunwales of his brother's boat midship, and held on tight while the rescuers paddled him away from danger.

There continued to be no safe place to land in the canyon, so with Brian still holding the side of the canoe Otto and Kevin turned their attention to pursuing the runaway torpedo. In another minute they had managed to catch up to a floating waterproof Pelican camera case trailing by a thin rope behind the upside-down canoe. Grabbing it and reeling in, they were able to reach the capsized boat, and hold on to its floating painter line. With the swimmer and canoe now both in tow, they urgently needed to land. It was unsafe to try to haul Brian out of the fast water into the fully loaded moving rescue boat, but clinging to the gunwales in the frigid water, he couldn't be expected to hold on much longer.

When Pat, Roger and I had gone to shore on river-left, Brian, Kevin, Otto and the capsized boat were a few hundred metres ahead of us, far over on the right. The closest land for them wasn't our side, but the edge of a long, low gravel island. Working hard they were able to manoeuvre their heavy load over to the island shore and whip the whole rig in safely to a gravel beach. This was where we had seen Brian walk out with Kevin.

A canoe full of water and gear is as heavy as a huge boulder. In order to firmly secure the boat in the shallows, Kevin had gotten out, and stood pulling with all his might on the bow line. Battling several signs of hypothermia, Brian forced himself to stand up in the shallow water nearby, and with shivering hands and shaky legs, tried his best to help by yanking on the stern line. Once the boat was firmly grounded, Brian told

Kevin that he just couldn't do any more. Exhausted and hypothermic he was helped onto land, and immediately sat down.

Nearly all of their gear had remained tethered in during the float. Once Brian was ashore, Kevin moved some of the gear out, and was then able to flip the partially loaded boat upright, and further lighten it by tilting, draining, and bailing. He hauled the much lighter canoe higher up onto shore, and went to work helping Brian. With Kevin assisting, Brian rested and fortunately recovered quickly.

As soon as Otto saw that Brian was safe with Kevin, he had taken off solo and made a short downriver dash in his canoe, trying to retrieve some items, including Brian's lost new Grey Owl paddle, a throwbag, and Brian's hat, the one which had lost its eagle feather back at Cache Creek. But these things were all gone with the current, and he returned back upriver to help Brian and Kevin.

———•———

On river-left Roger, Odile, Bert and I didn't know these details as we worked with Paddy, but at least we knew the two men were out of the water, and that there were rescue people and a boat with each of the cold swimmers. They were both alive and conscious, and Pat and Brian's boat seemed OK.

Bert and Odile's canoe was still nowhere to be seen, but we would have to deal with that later. All our people were safe. We had three out of four boats. As Paddy's health improved, and we watched the people across the river on the gravel bar island move around, we became fully convinced that Brian was going to be OK too. Kevin and Otto were no doubt experiencing the same sort of relief we were feeling with Pat.

A little over an hour after making it to shore, Pat was well enough to be able to walk slowly with Odile and Bert down along the gravel beach a half-kilometre, to a level area almost opposite the island where Brian, Kevin and Otto were. Roger and I hopped in our canoe and floated down to the same spot.

With a few paddle signals back and forth, it was all worked out. Brian and Pat's boat had been completely bailed, and the gear reloaded. Although shaky and pale, Brian was able to get back into the bow and paddle his own canoe, while Kevin took the place of Paddy in the stern. Otto paddled his boat solo close beside them as they carefully headed our way, front ferrying the 200 metres of fast moving river. We were a quiet but relieved bunch as we stood on the gravel beach below the remnant cliffs, watching them paddle over to join us.

They made the crossing easily, and were met with high-fives and paddlers' handshakes all around. After such frightening times through the long canyon, our group was quite relieved to be reunited. Pat and Brian were OK. So were Bert and Odile after their long hike. Very little gear had been lost from Pat and Brian's boat. Our resurrected, repaired Mary Ellen Carter the Second was sound and performing well. Still, no one underestimated how close we had come to tragedy. Things could so easily have gone terribly worse. Somehow grace had combined over and over with our skills on this difficult day.

But as we stood together, a kilometre down from the end of First Canyon, we were still in serious trouble. Pushed by the high-water, and maybe slammed repeatedly into rocks and other obstructions, the cargo of Bert and Odile's canoe could easily be spewed and gone. Even if we could find the boat, what shape would it be in? There was a good chance she would be wrecked, and irreparable this time. We also might search but never find her. Lost down some dead-end side channel, or buried beneath the water somewhere, the runaway could have simply vanished. We tried not to talk of worst case scenarios, but we all knew them, and could only hope for the best.

In the midst of this we noticed five mountain goats, including one with a tiny kid, way up high above us on the rock cliffs. Such a beautiful sight to see! Jody would love it! We had given the name Eagle Rock to the place where Roger and I had wiped out and then travelled on. When we saw the goats and that little baby, at this place where our group was now reunited, I thought to myself that maybe we should call this "Goat Cliff", "Kid Cliff," or maybe "Reunion Cliff." But none of these had quite the same ring to it, so I kept the idea to myself.

Looking around I noticed, a short way downriver on our side, a huge wide diagonal band of wine-red rock. It seemed to have been painted on the steep, grey cliff mountainside, but a gargantuan brush would have been needed to paint this swath. Like a massive single-coloured rainbow of stone, the burgundy left end pointed down, and touched our side of the river, while its right end pointed upwards, angled to the sky. In the distance, on the higher mountain behind it, the blaze continued on, going in the same direction, further and higher.

We had seen the leaning downriver, 45° rock motif continue throughout First Canyon, and also along the sides of this Goat Cliff. But the consistently tilted strata now seemed to be finishing, punctuated by this wine-red arc, as if it were some kind of exclamatory end mark. The leaning pattern ceased only a few hundred metres downriver from it. Whatever great upheaval these mountains and the canyon had gone through in the past, it looked like everything had made a huge change, right there. Though tense, worried, and tired, I was again filled with awe and a warm feeling, a kind of acceptance. There is beauty and mystery in nature everywhere.

My knowledge of geology isn't good enough to tell me what would have laid down this coloured swath, millennia before the mountains were thrust upwards, but the band remains there still, visible for all to see. Every rock layer above it and below it is grey, but that thick rainbow of rock is pure burgundy-red. The gravel beach where we stood is only a kilometre upriver from the place where this arc touches the Mountain River. If I ever come back, I'll know the spot.

After snacks we discussed the best way forward. Unlike the situation at Eagle Rock, we were not in a small canyon, nor in the middle of a long, dangerous stretch of rapids with a pinned boat right in front of us. Checking our maps and scanning through binoculars we could see that, with the ending of the canyon, we were now at the beginning of a long, wide, flood-plain valley, with many broad channels and low gravel islands. It looked like the moving water was going to be relatively safe: Class Two, for several kilometres.

Everyone was still reluctant to split the group. We compared different options and their risk factors. There was nothing for us to rescue yet, no wreck, no repairs to make. If we left any people here near this red rainbow cliff and the rest continued on to search, a return trip would be required to get them, whether we found the runaway boat or not. That return trip might be hazardous and difficult. What if the boats going ahead got into more trouble? There were definite hazards in leaving two or more people and some of the gear alone, either with or without a boat, for an indefinite time. Also, some of us were still shaky, needing support.

The alternative was to proceed with all eight people loaded into the three boats. This too would be dangerous. Carrying two extra people, in canoes that were already heavily loaded, would make each boat much more likely to tip. There were risks, but somehow we had to go on. We decided that maybe in these quieter waters we would be OK paddling this way for a while. We would take things slowly and proceed with care. Searching together, we would try to find the lost canoe.

We redistributed and balanced the weight in the three canoes. Each boat would have the same stern and bow paddler as usual. Adding the weight of Odile to the middle of one canoe and Bert to another, there would be three people per boat in two of our canoes. This would be partially offset by a reduced gear load in each of those canoes. The remaining canoe, the one with only two people, would carry its normal load, plus the extra displaced gear from the other boats. If problems arose, such as the difficulty level of the rapids increasing, or a weather change, we would have to pull over and re-evaluate. We didn't know how long we would be able to manage like this, but would start cautiously and see how things went.

After making the adjustments, our small fleet set off slowly downriver, all eyes gazing anxiously ahead and to both sides, scanning the water and shorelines. There was no need to remind anyone to be careful. We paddled as slowly as the current allowed, searching thoroughly for the canoe or any bits of loose gear, in every channel and eddy, along every beach and gravel bar island. We swept everything. Because we were searching so thoroughly, it took us three or four times the normal length of time to paddle the first kilometre, then the second, then the third.

Four kilometres from the red rainbow we finally saw in our binoculars a small pure black dot in the distance. Surging with hope, we headed for it. It looked like it might be the canoe, in an area off to the right, where there seemed to be a lot of floating fallen evergreen trees in the water. As we approached, the dot became an object. It was the right shape and size! Soon there could be no doubt. We had found her! Cheers let out!

But what condition would she be in? Our mixed emotions turned to complete joy as it became clear that this was indeed our boat, and she looked fully intact, having survived a free-wheeling run of about seven kilometres from the beginning of the canyon! Dropped by the river, where one of the countless gravel bars drained off to the right side, we found the canoe in shallow water, lodged on the roots of a full-sized, washed away black spruce. The boat was almost upside-down, and two thirds out of the water, lying broadside to the light current and the tree's root ball. One of its gunwales was lodged on the river bottom, and the open side was tilted upstream in the air at a 45° angle. Since the current in the runoff channel was quite weak, no buckling or flattening of the hull had happened this time. And the gear appeared to be still tethered in to the belly of the boat.

The spruce tree that had snagged her was fresh and green. It lay there roots and all, its spindly top pointing like a weather-vane in the direction the water was draining. There were also at least ten other full-sized green spruce trees spread along in the shallow waters, lying parallel every couple of metres, lodged on the gravel. All of these recent casualties had apparently been washed away from some upriver shore, perhaps together, maybe by the Eagle Rock floodwaters a few days ago. They had been floated down, then dropped here in the shallows by the lowering waters. For now, and perhaps only until the next big rain, these trees all lay there almost side by side, like a broad line of giant fallen soldiers. Somehow, earlier today, one of them had snagged our boat. Without being pinned, damaged, or held tightly in place in any way, our canoe had been left.

We quickly stashed our boats on the low gravel bar island beside the runoff channel. Standing on its shore we did a quick visual analysis. Everything looked stable. For a closer look I carefully waded into the knee-deep moving water. Placing each step slowly and deliberately on the gravel bottom, I was able to easily cross four metres to stand beside the canoe.

Thankfully the boat looked fine. The tether was still holding and all the gear seemed to be there. Bert waded in to join me and we tied three safety lines on the canoe; we didn't want to risk her getting away on us again. He took the ends of the ropes back across to the others, who walked a few metres upstream to get a good hauling angle, and positioned themselves, ready to pull.

The actual retrieval process turned out to be surprisingly fast and easy. While the lines were held tight, I stood beside the boat on the upriver side, and reached my right arm over the outermost end of the upturned bottom of the canoe, and underneath its downriver side. My hand was able to grab part of the midship gunwale there, near the place where it rested on the river bottom. Because there was barely any current, I was able to easily lift and roll the canoe in the upriver direction. In only a few seconds it was simply flipped and sitting upright. Although still completely swamped and very heavy with water and gear, she floated! Roger waded in, and held by our four hands and hauled by three ropes, we easily walked her over to the others on our gravel bar base. She was carefully emptied of all water and gear, and studied more thoroughly. We were astounded to see that there was no damage! The whole recovery had taken only twenty minutes. What an easy process compared to building a dam!

We could hardly believe our good fortune. Not only was the canoe in perfect shape, but nearly all of Bert and Odile's gear was still there. The only things missing were a spare aluminum paddle, the reflector oven, and our environmental stove. Amazing! The heavy metal items had no doubt gone permanently to the bottom of the river, but perhaps we might still recover the paddle.

Laughter and delight again took the place of tension and fear, and heartfelt paddlers' handshakes, high-fives and hugs were shared. Extremely pleased and thankful to have all of our people and all four of our boats back together again, we celebrated with a snack.

Perhaps encouraged by how Roger and I had done back in the big stuff in First Canyon, despite our resurrected, somewhat clunky, repaired canoe, the other three boats each added make-shift drop-sheet spray covers to their bows. Now we all had that little extra safety margin. The boats were loaded in our normal configuration, and we sailed off, leaving the line of fallen spruce soldiers to wait for some future high water ride.

For the next three hours the paddling was challenging and stressful. We were all tired and shaky, and proceeded with extra caution, ready to react. It had been a long, hard day since leaving Cache Creek, and everyone was worn down. First Canyon and its aftermath were behind us, but the waters were still quite swollen.

During a particularly challenging spell of several kilometres, the steep shoulder of a mountain came beside the swirling river's edge on the left. Fifty metre high cliffs lined the river as if the mountain had been chopped off. The right shoreline remained fairly low, with flat moving water, but the whole left half of the river near the cliffs had galloping haystacks. There also seemed to be shifting whirlpools. We got out on river-right and scouted with binoculars.

The usual skinny black spruce trees covered the cliff-tops on river-left, and continued marching up the mountainside towards the tree line. No longer leaning at a 45° angle, the rock strata lines of these steep cliff walls were now sometimes almost horizontal, and in other places the lines in the rocks seemed to swirl up and down, as if stirred by a giant spoon into a jumble of twists and turns. I again wondered at the incredible forces that must have caused this ancient record of changes, laid down over eons. We would pass by in minutes.

Staying away from the turbulence near the cliffs, we snuck our boats initially down the right shore, then steered back over to the main current, where it boosted us back up to high speed. Our canoes flew past several old shoreline willow trees, that were still standing and alive, but their thick trunks were immersed in more than half a metre of moving river.

We made it through the rest of the day without further mishaps. Despite the earlier, terribly close calls, and our fatigue and anxieties, we all did hours of fabulous whitewater paddling, running Class Three nearly all afternoon, and probably some Class Four. The three or four short sections of Class Two that we encountered were considered breaks.

We finally pulled our fleet in to shore on river-right, opposite a huge glacial fan of boulders that appeared to pour out of a V-shaped valley between two steep mountains, and our weary group made camp. The millions of white and grey rocks of the big fan made it appear at first glance as if it were the mouth of a glacier. But this fan wasn't made of snow or ice; it was made of billions of pebbles and boulders, a huge white river of stones.

What a day! Even with the rescues and all that happened, we still managed to travel 22 kilometres, including that incredible First Canyon. We now sleep at kilometre 179 from the Mackenzie. Tonight our camp is just six kilometres upriver from the famous Battleship Rock that we've seen in photos in Bill Mason's wonderful book, "Song of the Paddle." Almost immediately after that landmark island will come the entrance to Second Canyon. God I hope the rest of these canyons go better than the first! There are four more.

After our camp was set up I bathed in the river again, my first since Eagle Rock. It was still freezing cold, but again marvellous. We ate a hurried supper as a large, dark storm cloud moved in. It rained heavily for 45 minutes, which has given me time to write in the tent. But now it has stopped and I have to get up and bake tomorrow's bannock. Maybe those trees will be on the move again.

Thank goodness we made it safely through this day.

———•◆•———

13

I was given the gift of truly understanding the value of teamwork, more than I ever had. I am certainly not perfect. No-one on a team is perfect, and the team itself is not perfect. But the team gives strength, gives comfort, gives capabilities and endurance, gives insight, and even humour, that no single person can give. Our teamwork got us through the hardest times.

———•—•———

Before going to bed, I had made another little stick weir by the river. This morning, I saw that the level had gone down 30 centimetres as we slept, and so hoped this would perhaps give us an easier ride to Second Canyon and Battleship Rock. We only had six kilometres to go, but our maps showed us there would be a challenging early wake-up section. They were right. After launching at noon, our first hour was indeed very heavy going, through big rollers and side wash, but we were fresh and had a wonderful time.

A few kilometres later, in order to avoid large 70 metre cliffs on the left and strong currents swirling near them, our canoes stuck to the right, skinning along the edge of a gravel bar. After that we took a couple of sneak, low volume routes down secondary channels to avoid the biggest water, and arrived at our planned camping spot after only two and a half hours!

Along the way, the overcast skies slowly cleared. Waves of beautiful, undulating, deep blue cloud shadows washed over the river and mountainsides, alternating with spot lit sections of gold sunshine. The land's colours shifted and flowed, as if animated, and the air became fresh and dry. As a bonus, right on cue, at 1:00 the sun came fully out and stayed out! This provided us with a brilliant camp arrival at 2:30. After gobbling a late lunch, we savoured a wish come true: a warm, dry afternoon in camp.

Throwbag ropes were strung out as clotheslines, and we all hung up sleeping bags and large quantities of damp clothing. It was precious to have an extended time to relax, while at the same time getting everything drier than it had been in a long time. Bert and Odile especially welcomed the opportunity, since some water had leaked into their packs yesterday during their canoe's long float.

We are now camped 173 kilometres upstream from the Mackenzie. Our tents are pitched on river-left, only 100 metres before the opening into Second Canyon. Sitting in camp we can gaze almost directly into its mouth on the cliff-lined far shore. Directly opposite us, in the middle of the river, is the high rock island appropriately named Battleship Rock, or Ship Rock.

Silently standing on guard in the middle of the water, with wide, deep channels flying past on either side, this magnificent island is like a grand sculpture, a ship of stone. At six canoe-lengths long, and four wide at the broadest point, the ship narrows on its leading, bow end to a sharp prow. This points downriver, towards the canyon opening. On its blunt, stern end is an undercut cliff that no boat can safely approach. This abruptly deflects the entire main channel, splitting the river in two. The island's most dramatic feature is the fact that it towers four stories high, and is ringed with vertical cliffs. Standing slightly taller than it is long, Ship Rock gives the impression that if it were a real boat, it would be tall and somewhat stubby, with room for several decks. Way up on what would be the bridge, a few low bushes and three or four skinny black spruce somehow manage to hang on.

We all took full advantage of the down time, spreading out and recharging. The brilliance of the sun was further increased by a warm, almost silver yellow glow reflected off of both Ship Rock and the long wall of cliffs across the river. This line of vertical rock goes for about 200 metres and is broken only once, by the narrow door of the canyon's entrance. It was easy for me to daydream and imagine this tall Ship Rock somehow magically breaking loose, floating free of its rock ties, and sailing off downstream just a little bit, then slipping through that opening into the inside of the canyon. If it did, it would be almost a perfect fit, squeezing in with just a little water on either side.

After relaxing and a short siesta, some of us hiked down along the shore to get the best possible viewing angles into the canyon. It appears to be much easier than the last one, so we are optimistic. Brian did a bit more fishing, but again had no luck. For so many days now, the runoff from all the rain has made the river grey, and sometimes muddy brown. Today it has gone back to being cloudy and grey.

A few of the others went for a longer hike, high up the mountainside. They took photographs which they say will look as if they were taken from a plane. I was having a rest in our tent at the time, daydreaming of moving ships, but I wish I had gone with them. They said it was magnificent, with gorgeous vistas in every direction. I promised myself to nap less, and not miss the next opportunity to explore.

Kevin and I have a nice little robin's nest just outside our tent. This is the first robin I've seen on the whole trip. She's pretty quiet though, keeping her presence low key. She might have young. Relaxing in the tent I hear her wings flutter, and am reminded of Willow Handle.

———•———

14

The waters held us up, carried us, gave us beauty, thrills, peaceful times and nightmares.

———— • • ————

In the morning the river was down an amazing further half-metre, meaning that in two days the water level had dropped a total of 80 centimetres! Under clear skies we set off from Ship Rock just after 11:00.

As expected, Second Canyon was a much easier run than First. There was only one section of big turbulence, and it was on the first bend. A minute after I had taken my last look upstream back at the big ship, our strung out line of canoes slipped into the opening, entering from the left. As each boat came in, it turned around and front ferried towards the middle, then let the river push the bow gently back around, to aim downstream. Once in this position we just allowed the canoes to flow with the current, and rode a lovely train of splashing waves, enjoying the bouncing and bracing. From the last of these, we sailed into a thin channel on the left, just beside a gravel bar, and the rest was easy.

After leaving the canyon we paddled until mid-afternoon with only one break, running beautiful rapids and braided channels all the way. We often hugged the shore, enjoying rock dodging and manoeuvring. It was a five star day, with only a couple of spots where we had to hop out and pull our boats through shallow water.

Like yesterday, our travel time today was short, yet we went 23 kilometres. The scenery continues to be stunning, and several times Roger and I heard those soft clickity, clickity, clack sounds deep below as we paddled: the music of the river.

We've set up tonight at a spot where there are many big blocks of stone and rounded rock ledges. The grey blocks are roughly rectangular, but have somehow been made smooth, leaving them without any sharp corners. Many are stacked in rows, resembling Greek ruins. Our tents are pitched throughout them, in what look like the foundations of large, ancient rooms. The whole area also looks as if it could be some sort of grand scale rock garden, created by a master architect. But this masterpiece has been constructed by nature alone.

Across the river is a huge, broad cliff, which bends away from us as it rises, eventually reaching all the way to a mountain peak. It is magnificent, and has several distinct horizontal bands of colour. According to our map, the summit is over 250 metres above us. A stone rolling down would have a long trip to the river.

This morning in Second Canyon we passed another eagle's nest high on a cliff, but it looked unused. We didn't see any eagle. The immense cliff across from this evening's camp probably houses at least one big nest somewhere, but we have no way to get up there and take a look. Besides, I wouldn't want to disturb them.

Camped in the gorgeous riverside rock garden, at the base of this giant mountain, I am again awestruck by the natural world. I find myself thinking more about the mysteries of it all, wondering what can my tiny part be in this vastness? I don't often step inside a church, but the feelings that natural places like this stir in me make me believe I'm in a very special, gigantic holy sanctuary. Some might label it God, or a sacred place, or the house of God; some call it Nature; some the Creator, or the Great Spirit, or any one of hundreds of other names. To me the name doesn't matter. I just know that places like this draw something special and spiritual up inside of me, something primal that is usually kept sleeping on my inner back burner.

To my surprise I found myself remembering a hymn, even hearing it sung in my mind's ear. I used to sing it a long time ago, as a young boy, standing beside my mother and father in church. It's called "How Great Thou Art," and is a song that is formally addressed to God. But in my opinion, I've always thought the words could easily be switched to Nature. Part of the lyrics go:

When through the woods,
And forest glades I wander,
And hear the birds,
Sing sweetly in the trees;
When I look down,
From lofty mountain grandeur,
And hear the brook,
And feel the gentle breeze;

Then sings my soul…

Humming quietly to myself, I smiled to think that I should remember this here, and so clearly, from so many years ago.

Turning and looking back from the cliff and river to our camp, I saw two of the little resident varmints searching for scraps below one of our food barrels. By far the most common animals for the past several days have been these little ground squirrels. We didn't see any higher in the mountains, but now they seem abundant. Halfway in size between groundhogs and our small Ontario red squirrels, they repeatedly squeak and scold us, probably because we've set up our camp right in the middle of their home. We'll try not to make a mess, and will of course no trace the place when we leave, but I'm sure they'll be quite happy to see us go.

At noon today we passed the Stone Knife River, a major tributary washing in from a sweeping valley on the left. I was glad that it had at least been called a river this time, and not a creek! The Stone Knife is close in size to the Mountain, so their blended flow has made our river wider, deeper and, for now, much easier to paddle.

In the last three days we've travelled 51 kilometres from Cache Creek. Today we are camped just past the 150 kilometre point on our trip, and so are now exactly halfway to the Mackenzie. It has taken us 13 days to get here. Unfortunately, our delays have used up a lot of our planned exploring time. Still, if things go according to plan, we hope to be at the mouth of the Mountain River in only 4 more days, by the end of Day 17. That would make our rate of travel 13 days for our first 150 kilometres, and only 4 days for our second 150. Otto says we can do it, and I trust him. He has a lot of experience and knows these northern rivers much better than me. It's encouraging that our distance travelled has increased steadily each day.

There are some large haystacks and boils to get around first thing tomorrow but for now we're just enjoying ourselves, taking it easy in this beautiful place. We've eaten a late lunch, set up the tents, and have been basking in the sun, which has finally blazed down on us strongly for our first entire day. The clear early morning drifted into a long cloudless, warm afternoon. Now, at 5:00, there's still nothing but blue sky!

We've seen a few awfully big flies around this area. There aren't many, and thankfully they don't seem to bite. They look a lot like our Ontario house flies, except they're much bigger than either a deer fly or horse fly. The largest ones are longer than my thumbnail! Sometimes in the boat one would sail along with us, buzzing our heads lazily, until we could whack it away with a paddle, like a mini-baseball. But all in all the bugs have not been bad on this trip. I haven't needed to use my bug jacket at all. It's late afternoon now in the rock garden, the ancient ruins, and I'm writing lying in our tent with the screen door wide open. My legs are half out in the shade, yet nothing is biting.

I'll rest a little more, look over the maps again, go for a hike and scout the next bend, then eat a late supper and crash. I'm missing Jill, Jody, Daniel and Patrick an awful lot, and just took their pictures out for 20 minutes again, as I have almost every night. Like the weather, I seem to be writing about this pretty often.

I think about you so much. I'll be home soon. I love you.

———•◦•———

15

There was everyone being rescued, each person surviving their trials.

---·•◆•·---

Tuesday, July 23
Day 14

It's now two full weeks I've been away. This evening I built another little cairn of stones for Jill near camp. She's in my thoughts so often.

All morning we ran wonderful non-stop rapids in the sun, heading towards Third Canyon. Roger and I have become quite good with our communications, calling efficiently to each other to move our canoe quickly one way, then back, or to brace, watch out for a rock, or look out for a strong eddy line. It felt like we were running Class Three for hours, yet in some ways it was calm, almost like a form of meditation. My hands and forearms ache, but in a good way. This whole river is one long rapid!

After eating lunch on yet another gravel bar we all rested for an hour, lying flat on our backs, absorbing the warmth of the pebbles, almost asleep, with hats shading our faces, and our river-sprayed clothes drying on our bodies. When we eventually roused ourselves, we were ready for the canyon run. The maps told us this one would be lower and wider than either First or Second, so it was expected to be less dangerous. But unfortunately, although we started through at 3:30, we didn't finish the short 2.5 kilometre canyon run until 6:30, three hours later.

The first part went as planned. With our usual minute between boats, we ran the inside of the first big corner to the right, then zipped around a sweeping bend to the left, followed by a smooth back ferry over to the right again. Feeling pretty good about all that, we pulled our canoes in at a gravel beach, bailed a bit, and got out to scout.

Everyone walked across a big sweeping level corner, steaming in the hot sun in our paddling jackets, neoprene shorts and sloshing booties. From there we gazed downriver towards the last section of the canyon. It ended with a final big bend around a cliff. Our notes warned us of a 2.5 metre waterfall somewhere just upriver from where we stood, so after peering downriver as far as we could, we scouted all the way back to the canoes carefully, this time walking along the water's edge. The spot halfway back, which we thought must have been the place that had been called a waterfall, looked more like just a serious underwater ledge at the present high water level. But to be safe, we decided to line all our canoes around the bend anyway, until we passed the ledge.

With a rope on either end of each boat, we slowly walked our "horses" around the long corner. As always, we worked to stay focussed as we placed careful steps on countless rounded cobblestones and boulders, trying not to fall or turn an ankle on a roly-poly one. As the corner started to straighten after the ledge, we hopped back in, and ran the tight inside of the curve to the last shore eddy. This was beside the furthest downriver spot where we had stood scouting. We all eddied out there, and stepped out onto shore again for another look.

Next would come the part that we knew might be difficult: that last big bend. The river sped around a blind corner on the left as it went past the base of a high cliff, so that section couldn't be scouted. Each boat would have to go out of sight for a short time. We headed off nervously, but as it turned out, everything went fine. When we were almost all the way around the curve, we each eddied back out safely again, this time on river-left. Kevin was even able to catch a little video footage of the other boats rounding the corner.

According to our notes our destination campsite for the night was just ahead, around the last part of that bend, where the canyon was expected to open out. But when we rounded the bend we saw that before it widened there was a long, steep, straightaway, that ended with a big train of prancing white haystacks, just to the left of centre. Otto and Kevin were leading as usual, with Roger and I second. We saw them getting into some pretty big waves down there, popping up and down as they rode the fastest current line, 100 metres ahead of us. To avoid what looked like the roughest bumps, we slid our boat over a bit to the right.

Suddenly, their canoe was upside-down. They were in the water! We couldn't see what had happened, but assumed it must have been the large haystacks. Probably more surprised than us, they were both swimming behind their boat, right in the middle of the tallest waves. Our other two boats were a long way back. Roger and I knew it was up to us.

Paddling hard with my whistle in my teeth, I blew the three blast emergency signals repeatedly to tell the others, as we cranked our boat back over closer to the middle of the haystack line to get a stronger boost. We worked furiously to catch them without swamping our own canoe. Coming up were the same galloping waves that had just wiped out our strongest boat. They peaked at over a metre and a half. Learning from what we had just seen, we stayed off a bit to the side. The bobbing swimmers were being swept further towards river-left, closer to the cliff wall. This was not a safe place for them, or for us. At least the current there was slightly slower, and this helped us to gain on them.

After a couple of minutes of flat out pursuit we managed to catch up. I pitched my throwbag to Otto and clipped its rope to our stern thwart. Kevin managed to swim over and cling to our gunwale on the non-cliff side as we booted along. We tossed their paddles into our canoe. Otto held my line and was towed, floating a few metres behind. Somehow we also managed to get close to the capsized boat. Roger took over steering, and I was able to grab their trailing painter and clip it beside Otto's rope on our stern thwart. Now we had both people plus the heavy, semi-submerged canoe in tow. But all of us were still flying through big current and waves. The towed men were still in the icy water and at serious risk. We needed to get to shore somewhere fast!

Thankfully the canyon was just about to open, and there would be possible safe landing sites. Pumping as strongly as possible, we pulled left, out of the main current. A minute later, as the river spilled into the broad floodplain at the end of the canyon, we managed to haul ourselves, Otto, Kevin, and their boat over to a shore gravel bar and beach our canoe. While Roger secured us I jumped out, waded in to my knees, and helped Otto to his feet. He walked out on his own. Kevin too was able to get his footing and walk out. Thank God neither of them was hurt, although both were understandably shaken after their cold five minute swim. We turned their still-loaded canoe on edge in the shallows, partially drained it, and hauled it up on the gravel.

The canoe and gear were fine. As Otto came out of the water I saw with wonder and a smile that he still wore his hat, held on by the chinstrap. Also his huge eagle feather had stayed with him, still flying out behind. I was so glad the river hadn't taken it.

Kevin's hat too had stayed on his head. Even his sunglasses were still on his face as he walked out! Everything had happened so quickly! In all, I think the only thing lost was one of Otto's knee pads. Roger and I were extremely thankful at how things had worked out, and proud of the Class A rescue. But it was humbling and frightening that our group's situation had changed again, and so fast.

A few minutes later our other boats pulled in safely to join us on the gravel. Everyone helped quickly to get Otto and Kevin into warm clothes, and fully drained and uprighted their canoe. Then we all lined the four boats downriver the remaining half-kilometre to our planned camping spot. We had been so close! Camp was set up at an open place with flat rocks and a fine view looking back up to the end of the canyon. A big riverside bonfire was lit to warm the swimmers and comfort us all. We cooked and ate quietly.

I'm glad to be past Third Canyon. The magnificence of the chasm was unfortunately tempered by the danger at the end, but it was still gorgeous. Safely camped, I sat by the water's edge trying to pull my mind out of worry, back to more positive thoughts. We had been travelling through fabulous unspoiled natural beauty. Looking around me at the glorious views, I felt what I sometimes refer to as the "tripper's reward." This is the deep personal pleasure that only comes to a person when a goal is achieved by way of a difficult struggle. I thought to myself, "Nobody gets here by car."

There are two more canyons. Our notes describe them as shorter. Perhaps they'll be easier. We have three days left to get to the Mackenzie on time, with a total of 125 kilometres of paddling still to do. If things go as planned we'll travel 20 kilometres tomorrow, another 45 the next day, then on the last day we'll paddle our final 60 kilometres in the lowlands. The trip and wilderness experience have been incredible, and I'm so glad that I came, but especially after this latest fright, home is calling loudly.

Each one of our group's four boats has now capsized once. I pray there'll be no more dumps. Our salvaged and repaired Mary Ellen Carter the Second continues to perform well, and Roger and I have been able to help rescue the other canoes with her. We all know things could have been much more serious for every one of us. I have to keep my promise, and come home safe.

To get drinking water tonight I had to hike about a kilometre. Though it's starting to get a little clearer, the river remains silted and gritty. The water level is still dropping. I hope the fair weather stays.

It's now 10:50 p.m. Time to look at photos again and pass out. I still have no use for my flashlight, and probably didn't need to bring one.

p.s. We were passed at our camp tonight by two large Zodiac rafts and a guy in a kayak. We didn't ask where they had put in to start their trip, but learned that the kayaker hailed from South Carolina, and the people in the two Zodiac rafts were from Denver. In their much more bomb-proof boats they were averaging 35 miles per day (56 kilometres)!

16

I am left knowing that I've been to wondrous places, and done things I can hardly believe. I was there, did those things, saw those things, smelled that air, ran those waters.

———————

As the mouth of Fourth Canyon came into view, we pulled over onto yet another gravel bar for lunch. The sun continued to blaze wonderfully, as it had since our 10:30 a.m. launch. The morning paddle had been the usual combination of fun, hard work, and some adrenalin pumping times. We only needed to hop out twice to line, yet still there was hardly a moment to relax, or even bail, as we flew along, covering 17 of the day's planned 20 kilometres.

The cliffs flanking the entrance this time weren't as high as they had been at the start of the other three canyons. It seems to be the case that the walls of each successive canyon get a little lower. After eating, and scouting the best we could, our line of ducks headed slowly towards the gate.

Earlier in the morning we had leapfrogged the camp of the rafters and kayaker. They caught up again just as our lead canoe started into the canyon. Travelling faster than us, in their much more protected boats, they passed our canoes on the fly and disappeared around the first corner. Otto and Kevin followed.

After a couple of curves Roger and I came to a tight bend to the right. Remembering the dangers of getting caught on the outside of a fast curve, we did a solid back ferry, cutting across to take it on the inside. But there were hazards there too. Shortly after rounding the corner our canoe suddenly lurched, caught on the rising surface of large rolling boil. Like a stick floating on a pot of boiling water, we were lifted by some great unseen force. The bow rose almost a metre, while at the same time my stern began to be sucked down at the edge of the mound, into what was quickly transforming from boil to whirlpool. This water was alive!

It felt like our boat was pitched at almost a 45° angle. Poor Roger was perched above me, with the water twirling him and our bow, around and around. He paddled frantically, trying to haul the canoe up and out, and keep us from washing down the drain. Meanwhile, below him down in the hole I braced, steered and willed that canoe to climb back up. We couldn't lose her again! It felt as if we were hung there spinning and suspended for at least a full minute, though I'm sure it was less. Finally our frantic efforts paid off, and we were able to power up and over the lip. The boat popped clear, almost as if nothing had happened. The boil had rumbled off somewhere else, thank goodness, and the moving water around us became almost flat.

What would it have been like if we'd been sucked completely down, or capsized? Again feeling like car drivers who had experienced a four wheel skid and barely missed hitting a transport truck head on, we shook ourselves, said several expletives, and got on with the canyon run. We had come through unscathed. Thank goodness! I felt my partner had saved us.

As our canoe floated around a second hairpin turn to the left, we saw more boils beginning. Immediately pulling extra hard, we managed this time to manoeuvre the boat so that it only caught part of the edge of the expanding mound. Still, the boil continued to rise upwards like a giant bubble, perhaps a metre above the rest of the surface. We had to ride its rim, almost surfing, for several seconds. As if coming from some mythical underwater nine-headed hydra, the second head of water kept lifting, seeming to want to pitch us over and swallow us. Fortunately, we weren't raised as high this time, and it wasn't able to suck our stern into the forming whirlpool. Applying all that we had just learned, we were able to pull our canoe out unharmed, and immediately left the area before there was a chance for another head to pop up. With our hearts pumping, we zoomed around the next bend, powered over to the left shore, turned and stopped.

We couldn't see the action the others went through, but were relieved that in quick order our last two boats made it safely beside us. Roger and I cheered! A few seconds later the cliffs opened outwards on either side, and on the left dropped down to a lovely sandy beach area. Otto and Kevin were already there waiting. This would be our campsite. We set up on a low sand dune, beside a small cliff at the end of the canyon, and all relaxed in the sunshine. It was such a joy to be able to wander around in bare feet, feeling hot, dry sand underfoot and between my toes. I also felt a personal inner calm and increased but humble confidence: Roger and I had done well. In our battered, repaired boat, we had paddled on.

The fifth and last canyon is supposed to be easy. We have 45 kilometres to paddle tomorrow. Now let's have a safe finish.

In the afternoon I drew a sketch of part of camp. We are about to leave the highlands and go into the broad, flat flood-plain, the start of the Mackenzie River lowlands. All evening the sun has continued to bake down on us and everyone has really enjoyed lounging around. Our clothes and tents have gotten crispy dry. At 7:00 p.m. it's still far too hot to sleep in the tent, though sleeping is what my tired body seems to feel like doing. I'll gladly take a walk instead.

Edge of camp at the end of Fourth Canyon, river-left

– pencil, charcoal and conté sketch, Phil Weir

17

I'm more complete, more aware of my fragility, and more confident that good will indeed win out in the end.

———•◦•———

Tomorrow the Mackenzie!

Kevin and I slept with our outer tent doors open last night, leaving only the bug screen. Since it doesn't get truly dark, I was able to look out and enjoy a picture-perfect view of the lowlands. A short while ago, as I woke at 5:00 a.m. I watched a beautiful, brightening "sunrise" sky, with low horizontal bands of reddish orange, and deep purple. While enjoying the scene, I remembered the old saying: "Red sky at night, sailors' delight. Red sky in morning, sailors take warning." I wonder what kind of weather we are in for. Today is our 45 kilometre day.

Last night I hiked back upriver along the tops of the canyon walls, my most beautiful solo walk so far. I felt like a king, walking along surveying sweeping majestic views from the waterline to the mountain tops. I was able to look down, as if from the sky, on the giant bends and shifting boils we had paddled through: the waters travelled so far. The boils didn't look so big from that distance, and the whirlpools, hardly deep at all.

I was surprised to find a small metal building, roughly 3 x 3 x 3 m, with a solar panel and short antenna on its roof, and a few thick six centimetre wide cables going all the way down the cliff, and into the river. It was located high on river-left, just downstream from the biggest bend, and was almost certainly a water-level monitoring station. I wondered what sort of incredibly high readings it must have been getting lately. I made another little rock cairn for Jill, and shot a full roll of slide film, using Roger's camera this time. They'll be beautiful if they turn out.

While I've been writing, the morning sky has transformed dramatically. Bright orange and purple has now turned into deep, dark grey. So far it's not raining, but "Sailors take warning!" It's time to get up and make breakfast.

<hr>

Shortly after we ate, it did start raining. The weather changed completely from yesterday, turning back to cold and wet once again. We set off at 8:30 a.m. with drizzle and a chilly wind in our faces. Almost immediately the small remnant cliffs around camp dropped off to fairly level, spruce covered shores. Fifteen minutes after launching we made a brief pit stop at the camp of the Americans and chatted for a bit, all of us by then dripping extensively in full rain gear. We left them behind again and were boosted up to "warp speed" by the fast-forward current, covering an incredible 12 kilometres in the first hour! This is an amazing speed to maintain in a canoe, and we again had to keep alert and focussed. Even with the dank weather it was great fun, and the scenery spectacular.

Just after 10:00, as we paddled in our usual line, Roger and I followed Otto and Kevin through what looked like just another "V". But a surprise side-wash current came out of nowhere and pushed in hard from the right. We had suspected something might be coming, from seeing an unusual motion of Otto and Kevin's boat a short way ahead, but had barely enough time to turn our bow slightly towards it and brace with our paddles on both sides before it hit. The sudden bump lifted and jerked us, but we were OK. I quickly signalled with my paddle to warn Bert and Odile, travelling a few boat lengths behind, pointing for them to get over to the left to avoid the strongest impact of the side-wash. But at that particular moment they weren't looking, and missed the signal.

When the surprise push blind-sided them they were immediately in trouble. With no time to brace or manoeuvre, their boat was instantly bowled over. Odile and Bert were dumped into the cold water, shocked and swimming. Looking behind, Roger and I saw the boat roll upside-down, immediately stopped, and blasted emergency whistle signals.

As locations go for being spilled out of a canoe in remote wilderness, this unobstructed channel was a pretty good one. All our boats were close by. We had been travelling near shore, past the edge of a low gravel bar island. Pat and Brian had been following a short distance behind and were able to do a great quick rescue. They braced their own canoe through the side-wash, then caught the swimmers within seconds. Odile and Bert were both able to cling to the gunwales, and throwbags weren't needed. In less than three minutes they walked out unhurt on the pebble shore of the low island. In our stopped position, Roger and I simply let their capsized boat float to us, grabbed a floating line, and towed it over to the island, beside the others. Otto and Kevin heard the whistles and quickly paddled back up the shore to join us.

Though chilled and surprised, Odile and Bert were OK. Mainly they were just upset that this had happened. Their boat was fine, and once again, thanks to good tethering, no gear was lost.

The immediate priority was to build a quick fire and warm them, but in the continuing rain there was only sopping wet driftwood. A five minute group scramble to find any dry sticks brought nothing dry enough to use. Giving up on this method, I found a small soaking wet birch log, used my pocketknife to cut off its outer bark, and carved a few dry slivers from the inside. With these bits of shavings and a few flakes of inner, drier birch bark from another stick, we managed to get a little flame going. But it took ten minutes.

By that time Bert and Odile had gotten quite cold. Both were thoroughly drenched to the skin, plus the rain wasn't letting up. The rest of us were also getting increasingly shivery. We knew that in these conditions hypothermia could easily sneak up on them, and all of us.

Despite the quick rescue, everyone was unnerved that a dump could happen again, and so suddenly. While keeping an outwardly positive attitude as we worked through the recovery process, I couldn't help feeling reminded of our fragility, and of the need for constant, deep respect for the incredible power of natural forces. I glanced around as I worked making the fire. We were wet and vulnerable, in the cold rain, on a low gravel bar island, one of probably thousands of gravel bars, made of billions of stones, surrounded by water, in the middle of this vast wilderness. I was reminded of times when I have stargazed deeply into the sky's infinite space on clear nights and thought: we are specks.

Yet lovely pink fireweed plants were still there on this island of rounded stones, blooming away, even in the rain, each like a little local supernova. Spikes of low, northern-style, blue and white lupins also joined them here and there. I was struck by a thought which I found obvious, yet profound: every rock looks more gorgeous when it is wet. The philosophy of that sank in as I glanced up from fire lighting, and looked over at the river flying by, relentlessly heading to the sea. Water is so precious, in all its forms. The clouds above will swirl and change, and would not always rain. Just as surely, we would not always be here. We would move on. All of life is transient, but still incredibly dear. Rain makes rivers run. I again thought to myself: I must remember to look around more as I go, and enjoy every minute.

In the midst of this short time of reflection, while most of us were tensely trying to get our little fire going, there was a burst of unexpected humour. Just after the first tiny flame had flickered to life, Brian walked up looking for a light for his cigarette. Unaware of the fragility of our precious little fire, he bent over, casually picked up the only burning pieces of bark and wood chip, and proceeded to light his smoke with it! Aghast, we watched as the hard-won flame then promptly flickered out! We howled at him for what he had inadvertently done, and he backed away sheepishly to finish his puffing. We shook our heads and laughed, relit the flame, and laughed some more with huge belly laughs. In a few minutes we had a big, cozy bonfire. Everyone knew Brian would be teased about this for years. Laughing during tough times helps too. I would try to remember to smile more.

We made sure Bert and Odile were warmed and OK, and prepared their boat. After eating, we all climbed back in our canoes, and quietly re-launched.

Even with the spill, our fleet still managed to do our 45 kilometres today, thanks to the welcome current boost. At the end, Fifth Canyon turned out to be a simple, easy run, having no whitewater at all, only fast moving water. We cruised happily in to stop at a shore spot beside some hot springs, which had been eagerly anticipated throughout the cool wet day. Several of us immediately hopped into the largest pool, wearing our paddling clothes and all, and basked for a while in the lovely warm bath water. Another round of laughter, this time at how funny we looked, took the place of earlier worries.

After the first soak, we lined and paddled our canoes down half a kilometre to the campsite we had been told about, on river-left, and set up. Everyone then walked back up the shoreline for a proper, and very satisfying, hot springs bath, this time without paddling garb. With wisps of steam rising from the pool, and a light sulphur smell in the air, we leaned back and relaxed in nature's spa, calling it the "Mountain River Hot Tub." Joking, and telling stories, we looked around at the beautiful surroundings, as all the while the river flowed past right beside us.

Now, I'm relaxed and exhausted. But after a short rest I have to get up and cook supper. This is our last camp duty day. Then tomorrow, on our last canoe travel day, Roger and I will be off!

We've now passed through the last of the canyons. I'm sure the remaining 60 kilometres to the Mackenzie River will be challenging, but it should be less dangerous. Even after all our group's trials, it looks like we'll be back on time, with everyone safe and sound. It's been a miserable weather day, but as we made camp this afternoon the wind and rain let up. We all hope for a sunny finish.

For the past two days there's been no good drinking water anywhere near our camps, and we've had to filter the thick silt out of the river water, using coffee filters. Even so, it still tastes a little gritty and has been dubbed "Mountain River Special Blend."

Our river-mates in their rafts and kayak pulled in at around 6:30 p.m. for another short visit. We chatted and shared some cheese and crackers before they sailed on ahead. After supper Brian went fishing again, but still saw no fish. The water's too cloudy. Yet he seems happy just to stand in this beautiful place and try. Who needs actual fish?

In many ways Brian's cheerful, mellow personality on this trip has shown me that, from his perspective, things have not been as stressful for him as they have been for me. Perhaps this is true for some of the others too. A person's outlook, point of view, and circumstances make a big difference to their feelings. Eight people on a trip means that there are eight different trip experiences, sets of memories, and ways of perceiving. I could only really know mine. Brian was loving the trip. Despite our tense times and close calls, so was I. A few people back home might find it hard to understand, but even given all our difficulties, I would still love to do this trip another time, if I ever get the chance. I again thought of Michael Peter Smith's song:

> Some day...
> In the rain...
> In the sun...
> I will see you again…
> Some day...
> Some time...
> Or never…
>
> ….We are here for a moment, then gone…to sometime…or never.

I ended the evening with another of my precious solo walks. Wandering up the gravel floor of the canyon towards the hot springs, my gaze and thoughts floated across the millions of polished pebbles washed to this particular place, at this particular time, by this river. Coming from somewhere upstream, maybe even from the top of some cliff or mountain up there, each had somehow tumbled their way here, been rounded over time, gone through who knows what, and had become smoother. Probably they had also clickity, clickity clacked their way along the bottom. They might sit on this gravel beach for a day, a year, maybe a thousand years. Then eventually, somehow they would roll their way onwards, heading towards the sea. Our group would stay just one night, and be gone.

When my wandering reached the warm sulphur springs creek I thought of how the spring and the river both flowed on, regardless of whether or not any people were nearby. I sat a while quietly, just looking around. In the midst of the river valley, full of rocks and rushing cold water, green algae grew midstream of the hot spring, exactly where the water was warmest. Nature doesn't miss a trick. I again thought of my young scientist daughter, and how she would be fascinated.

God I miss you all! – Time to look at your pictures. See you real soon.

18

I think there is something in Zen Buddhism about seeing all of the world in a grain of sand. The river's pebbles were a universe.

----•-•----

Friday, July 26 – evening
Day 17 on-the-river
The Mackenzie at last!

We're here! Our camp is on the level confluence corner where the river-left shore of the mighty Mackenzie River meets the river-right shore of the Mountain River. A few metres to the north, the wide, and now slow moving, Mountain blends its waters into the Mackenzie. Fort Good Hope is roughly 70 kilometres downriver on the Mackenzie to the north. Norman Wells is upriver 100 kilometres. For tonight, we are still in the vast wilderness, with no signs of any past or present human activities, except in our campsite area.

We have come from source to destination! From here the combined waters of these amazing rivers will continue northward to the Beaufort Sea and Arctic Ocean, being joined along the way by the waters of several more rivers. Here, at its mouth, the broad opening of the Mountain River is over 250 metres wide: a quarter of a kilometre. Far across the huge expanse of the much wider Mackenzie, it is 1,500 metres to the east shore: a kilometre and a half!

Water is everywhere. Looking out over the Mackenzie's surface, I see mountains on the far side. I'm can hear the low frequency downstream rumble of the great Sans Sault Rapids, which span the entire Mackenzie only a couple of kilometres to the north. Far out on the smooth water, big herring gulls are calling. Small terns wheel and cry up above. We are at the great river, and it is such a different world. Far from the closeness and uncertainty of the canyons, we rest in the middle of this immense open space, surrounded by omnipresent change and power. If this water were briny, we would be beside an arm of the ocean.

After paddling 19 kilometres in the morning, we stopped for snacks and filled our water bottles at a clear little waterfall. Just after that we saw our first seagull since leaving Norman Wells. This became a trend as gulls became increasingly frequent, just like when one is nearing the seashore. Relaxed cruising became easy, with only a couple of moments of excitement. In one of these, a few 1.25 metre high waves suddenly rolled underneath us, coming seemingly from out of nowhere. But our canoes just lifted and lowered back down over each of them. All in all, it's been a calm, steady day. We even rafted up all four boats for twenty minutes, only the second time on our trip.

With each kilometre travelled, the remaining cliffs and hills on either side receded further into the distance, until the entire landscape flattened out. Like an unravelling sweetgrass braid the intertwined channels of the Mountain River got wider and wider as the whole waterway broadened and slowed down.

Though straightforward, the day was long. We put in at 9:30 a.m., and stopped for lunch around 1:00. After eating we were sitting around, many of us lying flat out on the rounded cobblestones of another gravel beach. I was practically asleep when someone shouted, "Bear! Over there!" With a zing of adrenalin we all jumped up, grabbed our stuff and headed back to the boats on the double. It was an adult black bear, about 100 metres upstream, walking in our direction along the edge of the shoreline bushes. But between us and the bear was Brian!

Later he told us he'd gone up the shore alone to have a smoke, which he usually did in polite consideration of the rest of us. He had then gone into the bushes to relieve himself, and was on his way back, walking along the water's edge, when he too heard someone yell, "Bear! Over there!" Looking up, he saw us all gesturing frantically for him to look behind, as we quickly loaded our canoes. He wheeled and saw the bear, and then a second one, which came out of the bushes behind the first one! These bears were a lot closer to him than they were to us. Brian raised his leg, as if to start running towards the boats, but we saw that, in a split second of extreme self-control, he must have realized, mid-air, that this might not be the best way to act in front of a couple of bears. He instantly switched to a brisk walk instead. Hustling as fast as he could, he soon made it to the boats. Once he was safe, everyone had a great laugh.

Knowing that we were out of danger, and everything was stowed, ready to escape in a flash on the water, we stood a while by our canoes, just watching. The bears skirted nervously around the area where we had been sitting, keeping a cautious distance. They were probably there simply because this area was on their preferred normal route of travel, more than out of any real interest in us. They seemed to be slightly curious, but not at all aggressive. We had fun getting great shots with our cameras, with no need or wish for a gun. Our air horn and pepper spray were there, if needed to scare them away, but as is usually the case, these bears were much more afraid of us than the other way around. From our safe vantage point, we watched as they quietly loped away, into the willow bushes. Like my flashlight, the air horn and pepper spray ended up being good precautions to have along, but they were never needed.

I felt quite conscious that this was their neighbourhood, their home, not ours. We were the oddities passing through, the main source of potential danger. If it had been a grizzly or two, it would have been a different story. We would have immediately gotten into our boats and be gone in a flash. But these black bears didn't want to bother us, or even come near. It was special to have the chance to watch them. I thought of how all three of my kids would love this. I also chuckled, thinking of the great story Brian would have to tell.

Earlier in the day, Roger and I also saw two large river otters. They were almost beaver-sized, but slimmer. After climbing out of the river and up onto the bank, they saw us, and quickly dove back in without making a splash. A few seconds later they popped their heads up and looked back at us, like twin periscopes. Later we saw three young Canada Geese on a beach of black sand. They couldn't fly yet, being only about half-size. There's so much more wildlife on this floodplain than there was in the mountains.

My favourite sighting happened only three kilometres from the river's mouth. As we neared the end of our journey, a mature bald eagle lifted from a black spruce just ahead of the lead boat. It circled slowly, rising, its brilliant white head and tail shining, until at last it was very high, directly above us all as we paddled along. Both Roger and I took this as another positive omen. To be sure, there are many people who don't attribute any special significance to this sort of event, but I believe there is more complexity, richness and mystery in this world than we can possibly understand or even imagine. Whether it comes from inside my brain, that I attribute something special to the bird and the event, or whether there actually is real magic happening out there in the world, it makes no difference to me: when wonderful things occur, special is undeniably special.

The river continued widening and slowing for the final few kilometres. By the end, the muddy, meandering delta had almost completely flattened out. No longer a tumbling, roaring escalator on fast-forward, she had become a very different Mountain River. Our boats glided softly to the lip of her mouth, touching it at 5:00 p.m.

Stepping out, there were celebratory, triumphant paddlers' handshakes, hugs, pats on the back, laughter and sighs. We savoured the sweet completion of our trip, and our strenuous, successful day's paddle of 60 kilometres. It was a relaxed end to a very busy 302 kilometre journey. We looked at each other, smiling with knowing trippers' eyes. We had done it!

Our canoes were welcomed by our kayaker-rafter buddies, and we all lined up proudly for them to take our end-of-the-trip group photo. Click! There we all were: grinning, looking very woodsy, suntanned, more experienced, and most of us quite a bit hairier than we had been in front of the museum in Norman Wells. Everyone was happy and elated. I felt a wonderful, almost dreamlike feeling. We all spent what seemed like an hour just standing around, almost in a daze, aimlessly wandering the shore, decompressing, enjoying being at our destination. Then we all got busy and set up the last group camp.

Now, I am resting in our tent. It's 7:45 p.m. I'm safe, sound, dry and comfy by the shore of the Mackenzie. It is the end of Day 17 on-the-river, Day 18 of the entire trip. Our big celebration supper is coming right up. Tomorrow at noon we'll be picked up by motor boat by Frank Pope, our outfitter. Just before then, at 10:00 a.m., our kayaker-rafter friends will catch a Porter float plane out. Maybe it will be the same little Platypus that carried Roger and I.

As I lie relaxing, I think more deeply about this day, our last on the Mountain River. All the way along today we saw countless silent, floating trees, and beached uprooted ones. Some were snagged on mud or sand, some on rocks. Nearly all of them were still vivid green. Only days ago, each of them had been standing somewhere, living. It was life in motion, and death too. All part of the river, the land, the sky: part of Mother Earth. Each had somehow been washed away from its home. Somewhere upriver, in the past few days, probably during the Eagle Rock flood, possibly near us, or maybe somewhere far away, each of those trees had fallen in and been swept along, as we too were carried by these waters.

We are all connected. We are all related.
Everything is connected. Everything is related.

– Ginawaydaganuc.

We have much to be thankful for.

– Meegwetch.

I'm so glad to have done this river! And I'm also glad to be done! I feel full and empty at the same time, exhausted but also fulfilled. It's been a truly marvellous adventure, but taxing to the limit. Many times it was quite scary. I certainly profoundly respect this Mountain River.

Chatting around our big crackling bonfire this evening the group decided that we had actually paddled seven canyons in total, including the five major ones on the Mountain, plus the two smaller ones on Black Feather Creek: the first "Not-a-canyon," and also the "Eagle Rock Canyon." Except for the final 20 kilometres, the entire 302 kilometres of this river has seemed like one long rapid. Under normal weather conditions, the moving water experienced on this trip is usually rated as mainly Class One and Two, with some Class Three. But we rode her during a big-time flood, and because of the high water volume and other risk factors, we believe that we paddled Class Three most of the way, with some Class Two and even a little Class Four. What a ride!

After dinner I went for a walk with Kevin. We again searched for half an hour trying to find clear drinking water, but couldn't find any that was silt-free enough to be drinkable. We ended up using our coffee filters again to make our "Special Blend". Even after filtering, it still looked like tea. Later on, some of the others drank a little scotch, which was almost the same colour.

We sat on big driftwood logs around a huge bonfire, laughing and sharing memories, enjoying the long evening together. There are so many good feelings now. Everyone has relaxed. It's a big strain to do a trip like this, especially for the trip leader, and Otto did a super job. Despite the many challenges, all of us came through with flying colours. And yes, we are still talking to each other. I hope the weather is good for our four hour, 100 kilometre motorboat ride tomorrow, back up to Norman Wells.

It's now midnight on the Mackenzie. Gulls are cooing quietly on the water. The big rapids rumble on loudly down below. It's time to sleep and dream of talking to you all on the phone tomorrow. That will be the highlight of the trip.

———

19

Where was I when I started? Where was I at the end? Where am I now?

You go to places you never dreamed of going, just by going out in a boat.

It's 8:45 am and quiet beside the two rivers. Outside our tent everything looks soft and grey. The waters of both rivers seem to be in a flat calm, and make no sound. So far, camp is still asleep.

Light rain is starting to fall one more time. Of our 18 trip days, there have been only four with no rain. Except for three and a half sunny days, it's always been cool, and often cold. Many nights I needed my sleeping bag hood drawstring done up. I've found it to be warmest sleeping naked, except for my red touque and purple fleece headband, which I occasionally pulled down and wore as an eye mask, to make it seem dark. I often thought how funny I would look to someone who saw me get up to pee. Of course we all look pretty funny these days. I've alternated with my two pairs of long john tops and bottoms underneath everything for at least part of every single day, and have washed them (intentionally) four times. Thank goodness for layers.

A few metres behind our tent to the north, the Mountain flows in. Some of that water has travelled all the way from Willow Handle Lake, like us. Every drop, from every tributary, hillside and little stream, first came from the sky. Once clear, now cloudy and brown, the swollen waters softly blend into the waters of the Mackenzie. We are at their great meeting place. Throughout time, other people must have met here too.

It seems strangely quiet on this last morning, as I try to listen more carefully from my sleeping bag, in my home-away-from-home for the past 17 nights. Everything is silent. For the first morning since the source lake, no sound of moving water can be heard, except the distant low rumble of the Sans Sault. What a pair of rivers these are! From here their waters head north towards Inuvik, and will eventually spill into the Beaufort Sea and the Arctic Ocean, over 500 kilometres downstream! Our group will head the other way, southward, homeward.

I lie and think about that for a while as I hear a few people getting up, talking in low voices, rattling pots. I remember my first morning on Willow Handle, and consider maybe going for a little solo walk in the rain. But the coziness of my sleeping bag wins out this time. I decide to stay in bed in bed for one last camp morning by these incredible rivers.

I think over our wildlife sightings, and write out a list:

There were the little, quietly chirping birds in the shore bushes surrounding Willow Handle. Perhaps they were some sort of sparrow or warbler. I remember them best for the sound of their small wings fluttering intermittently in the silence.

The most common birds were the small, peeping spotted sandpipers that we often saw by the water's edge. These little grey birds, with their white and speckled bellies, would stand bobbing their heads and bodies, then fly off peeping in a flight pattern of distinctive lilting and tilting. We saw them all the way along on our journey, by both calm shores and rapids, even in places where there were no other birds. A few terns were seen, but only on the upper lake, and here at the Mackenzie, nowhere in between. Upriver from First Canyon we saw four or five spruce grouse, and just before Second Canyon, opposite Ship Rock, Kevin and I were treated to that single nesting robin by our tent.

We saw hardly any large wildlife, although we did see lots of tracks. For example, here on this Mackenzie beach yesterday were what looked like large wolf tracks. Moose scat and their tracks were found almost everywhere there was mud, sand or soft earth, but we saw only one moose. From their lead boat on Day 4, Otto and Kevin spotted some caribou up ahead on shore, but they were gone by the time the rest of us got there. At the Golf Course some of the others saw a wolverine, but I missed it. Mountain Goats were seen, but only the one time, near the big red rainbow cliff. And there was that cameo appearance of the two black bears.

Most memorable for me were the two eagles: the unforgettable golden eagle circling above us all at Eagle Rock just as our boat came free; and the end-of-trip bald eagle lifting from the riverside spruce, and then circling high above us, just before all four of our boats paddled safely home to the river's mouth.

Perhaps if our weather had been drier we might have seen more big animals and birds, but during most of our time on the river, the swollen water's edge was a precarious place to be. No, the wildlife wasn't the outstanding feature of this trip: it was the water, in all of its many forms.

I roll around stretching a few last times in my sleeping bag, and think to myself with a smile, "I do love camping, but tonight, I'll be in a lovely, soft, real bed!"

———•◦•———

We're back in town. The motor-boat ride back up the huge Mackenzie to Norman Wells was a hoot! Such a different way to travel compared to human-powered boats.

In the morning, after doing our last camp pack-up, we saw our rafter-kayaker friends off in the little plane. The pilot told us he had flown over three motor boats coming towards us, about an hour away by water. This would be Frank Pope and his two assistants, coming to shuttle us back to Norman Wells in his two 16 foot power boats with their 40 horsepower motors, plus one big 18 footer with an 85.

They touched the shore by the mouth of the Mountain River at exactly 12:05 p.m., only 5 minutes late from our pre-arranged rendezvous time. Not bad! It was wonderful to see them. In what we all considered was a very nice touch, they immediately passed around cold beers.

While loading we chatted with two fishermen who had pulled in off the Mackenzie, coming up from the north in a Zodiac. They were oil workers from Norman Wells, on holiday, returning from near Fort Good Hope. They had caught fish, despite the weather, by fishing the far shore tributaries down-river. The waters there were much clearer, because they came in from eastern areas, where it hadn't rained as much.

When Pope saw our Mary Ellen Carter the Second he just shook his head in wonder. Hearing our story he was amazed that we had been able to retrieve it and repair it, and that it had been made, not only seaworthy and trustworthy for our long journey, but had also performed really well. To his lasting credit he never once mentioned us paying for any damages. These northerners really understand what it's like out there, and he was just relieved that we were OK. The group gave him some gifts: our Coleman repair kit, and a big leftover salami. We also promised to send him some of our trip pictures, a video, and letters.

Frank and his assistants went to work and stashed two of our four black Coleman canoes in the bushes, just up the Mackenzie shore. These were swapped for two tripping canoes that had been left hidden there for him by a previous Black Feather group. He said he would get his last two Colemans later, on another trip.

Just before we finished loading, I took a quick walk over to the mouth of the Mountain River, cut off a piece of my sweetgrass braid, and dropped it in the water: Meegwetch! I then hurried back to the group. We finished no tracing the place, loaded, did a final sweep to make sure nothing was forgotten, and hopped in.

Two of the motor boats each took three of our people, and one took two. The one that only took two also took all four canoes. Frank's two black Colemans were tied right way up, suspended above the water on long spruce pole pontoons that crossed the boat and jutted out on either side, about half a metre from the gunwales.

Our Mary Ellen Carter the Second was one of the boats left behind for later retrieval. Too late, as I took my last look back from the departing motor boat to the places gone by, I realized that I hadn't said goodbye.

As the morning had gone on, the wind had come up, and the Mackenzie changed from calm to quite choppy. The two

Black Feather canoes were towed in the water behind the boat on a rope, splashing and often almost flying. From the speed and repeated slamming of the waves, their tow-rope broke twice, and had to be repaired during brief mid-river stops. Also, a thwart on one of the towed canoes broke loose on one side. The Mackenzie was showing its might, with big rolling and breaking waves, and lots of large debris to dodge.

I rode in Frank's boat, the big 18 footer, with Otto and Pat and piles of gear. We ploughed and hopped our way up the huge river in flood, while the waves came crashing head on. These were nearly always at least a metre high, but in some sections they rose to a metre and a half. The immense waterway broadened further, becoming five kilometres wide in some places. It never narrowed to less than a kilometre and a half.

After an hour, it started to rain – of course! Then, for the remaining three hours we travelled in wind, rain, and high seas. It was like going 100 kilometres on a wild midway flume ride, except these were much bigger waves, and there was a lot more hopping and crashing on today's ride.

When we got to town, Otto, Roger and I opted for splitting a hotel room three ways instead of camping in the sopping wet municipal campsite beside the river. I'm so glad we did! The others chose to camp, and unfortunately had another very soggy, windy night. Our room's hot shower, soap and lovely toilet were very popular.

When we came into the restaurant for the first time we surely looked a sight! The locals just smiled and said, "Rough day out on the river, eh?" We wolfed back enormous dinners and four bottles of wine. Then the three of us went back to our room while the riverside campers continued in the restaurant. We heard in the morning that between them, they downed an additional bottle of scotch and a twelve pack of beer. But it might have been bravado.

In the middle of all this, I got to phone home. It was so wonderful to talk to Jill. I cried.

Roger and Otto slept in the two lovely single beds. I drew the short straw and slept on the floor, snug and dry on my Therm-a-Rest, cozy in my sleeping bag, with a real hotel pillow under my head. I was quite content. There was no need for me to wear my toque or headband. It felt great to be squeaky clean, comfortable, warm and dry.

I drifted off smiling, thinking of the river, and home.

.

20

Otto came back with his eagle feather, Roger his moose horn, I some rocks and pebbles. But inside I came back stronger, prouder, and also more humble.

I'm more aware, more caring, about what Indigenous peoples call "Our Mother." How can we not care for her? She sustains us all.

───•─•───

Sunday, July 28
Day 20 on the entire trip
Layover day in Norman Wells

From the start of our planning a year ago, we had scheduled this extra layover day. It's always a good idea on long trips to leave some room for unforeseen developments and delays, and to prevent unsafe rushing. We were happy and proud that, despite our many adventures and delays, our group had arrived at the destination on time, without actually needing this safety day.

Some of us woke up in a nice dry hotel room, and some in wet riverside tents. Besides the continuing rain, there was also a blustery wind, which we heard had broken one of Bert and Odile's tent poles in the night. It was still cold, and stayed that way all day. "Mountain River weather," we started calling it. The wet, cool stuff just wasn't going to let up.

Most of us got together in the hotel restaurant in the morning, snug and dry. Our big breakfast was perfect: cooked by someone else, cleaned up by someone else, and eaten until we were stuffed, while we all sat on real chairs at real tables. Luxury!

I drank almost a full pot of coffee, and it tasted so good! This was partly because we had been forced for the last four days to ration our coffee to only one cup each, since we were almost out of fresh grounds. Yesterday, on the very last morning, while camped by the confluence of the Mountain and the Mackenzie, there were no new grounds left. This meant that everyone had to either drink my "extra special" batch, made from recycled coffee grounds, or not drink any coffee at all. I brewed this by re-using the wet grounds that I had been saving up in a plastic bread bag for the last four days of rationing. Despite a lot of teasing, everyone seemed to accept it. This coffee rationing and re-using had seen us through to the end of our trip, and had been better than nothing, but it was wonderful to get back to the real thing!

Because it was Sunday, the little town was mainly closed and sleepy. There had been a big wedding the night before, and we were told this was the first one in town in ten years! It was held at the Legion, a beautiful log building. The yard had been full of pickup trucks and vans coming from all around. Most people up here drive these big vehicles. We've only seen a handful of cars.

The excellent little Norman Wells Museum was open and we enjoyed touring it again. It was even more meaningful than before our paddle. They were showing the *Man Alive* TV series film about Bill Mason. This was totally fitting, since the Mountain River had been one of his favourites, and also he and his works had helped inspire us to do this trip. As we left, we joked that our Mary Ellen Carter the Second should be put on display in front of the museum, perhaps as a cautionary exhibit.

As the day went along I drew inward, keeping my thoughts to myself, feeling melancholy a lot of the time because I wasn't with Jill. It was our wedding anniversary. For the past eighteen years we had always been together on this, our special day. But for today, our number nineteen, I was such a long way away. Still, it was fantastic to talk to her again on the phone in the morning, and later to Jody, Daniel, and Patrick. It was so good to hear their voices! I wished I didn't have to wait a day to fly out, but knew I would be with them soon. We would have lots to catch up on, so many stories to tell.

Roger was flying to Edmonton to visit his brother for a few days on his northern Alberta farm, on the way back to Ottawa. He was lucky, able to change his arrangements and fly out today. Understandably he was happy to be on his way without lingering another day in town. Town was fine, but our wilderness journey had been what the trip was all about. Now it was time to move on. I was envious but happy for him as I walked with him to the small airport.

We talked of the wild times and the good times. So many good times! He said he was going to put the giant moose horn in his garden at home. I saw him off with a strong paddlers' handshake, a bear-hug and, "So long partner! We made it!"

Yes, we sure did! We had travelled together on an incredible journey, a fantastic experience.

Each and every one of the eight of us had been very lucky in our own ways, but I still believe Roger and I were the luckiest. Adversity was certainly often present, but so were many blessings, much wonder, joy, faith, and laughter – rich full laughter. Some kind of grace was surely always right there with us. "And, like the Mary Ellen Carter" – we rose again!

The rest of our group enjoyed the remainder of the day and evening in town, including a fabulous four hour dinner where I ate delicious fresh trout and the others ate caribou. Pleasant conversations were shared all round. In the restaurant we also talked with six Finns who were restless and worried. They had been delayed, held in by the weather from starting their own canoe trip on the nearby Natla-Keele River. They had come for only eleven days, and so far had lost two. The weather was too rough to fly the Twin Otter. We could relate.

Back at the hotel I crashed at 11:30, this time sleeping in the real bed vacated by Roger. So very soft!

What an unusual anniversary.

———•◆•———

21

I was given the gift of confidence – confidence to get out there and go, again and again, on other waters. Many other places in my life would never have been seen if it weren't for our Mountain River trip.

―――•+•―――

Monday, July 29
Day 21
Leaving for home

By 9:00 a.m. the riverside campers and the hotel crew had eagerly packed and were ready. We then relaxed for the rest of the morning, chatting with interesting local folks. Perhaps it's the isolation, or maybe it's because each person has had to work so hard just to get here, but everyone we saw smiled and waved or chatted: great Northern Hospitality!

Otto went and got an export permit for his big eagle feather. He had to fill in a lot of paperwork because it came from an endangered and very special species. It's good they keep an eye on these things.

At 2:00 Frank picked up the seven of us and all of our gear, from the waterfront and the hotel. The mighty Mackenzie River, which was already loaded with debris when we came up her the day before yesterday, was now quite a bit fuller, and had also become studded with many more floating and semi-submerged hazards. These included thousands of full-sized trees, more fallen soldiers in the giant wet parade, all moving along as if in a straggling log drive. But like the spruce that had snagged Bert and Odile's canoe, these trees had not been felled by people. The rain and high waters had somehow washed them away from where they had grown, and now they were floating down the huge swollen river with their roots, green branches, and all. They and all of the other miscellaneous large pieces of debris created a wondrous sight, but also a serious navigation hazard. No boat could possibly go out there in these conditions.

Word went around town that the mighty Mackenzie River, that vast moving body of water, had risen a full vertical foot (30 centimetres) in the past couple of days from all the recent rain water washing in from its many tributaries. That's one huge volume of water!

If it hadn't been for our extra layover day, we probably wouldn't have been able to get back up the Mackenzie to Norman Wells a day later. Held in by the increased hazardous debris, we would have been waylaid at the mouth of the Mountain, and perhaps not been able to get home for two or three more days. Flights would have had to be rebooked. Families would have been worried. Once again we realized our good fortune.

In the late afternoon, we caught our jet and flew out, southbound, towards Ottawa, via Yellowknife and Edmonton. The plane lifted off, and almost right away did a big bank turn to the south. We watched the small airport fall away below, then the town and outbuildings of Norman Wells. Everyone in the plane was pretty quiet. As it made its sweeping turn, we could see the mighty Mackenzie, the broad floodplain, then the mountains, those beautiful Mackenzie Mountains. They rose up sharply, towards Willow Handle Lake, the Continental Divide, and the sky. It was my last look upstream for this trip, to the places gone by. I was full of mixed feelings.

When things levelled off and my emotions settled a bit, I found myself focussing on the loud wall of sound surrounding me in the plane. To my tripper's ears the hiss of air inside and outside the jet sounded a little like amplified, relentless white-water. Except this would be whitewater travelled in a huge rumbling truck with bumps, along a vast river made of air. With a twinge of sadness I felt my connection with the natural world weaken. I thought to myself that perhaps everyone on the plane might be feeling something similar.

We were all still part of nature of course. This would never change. But the human-centred, human-dominated milieu was back now. There were no birds fluttering nearby in the bushes, no paddle swirls in the water, no wet river gemstones, no smell of spruce. All of that seemed gone for now, replaced to some extent with the wondrous clouds outside my window, which I realized were magnificent as well, and really just another form of white water. The sky and aerial perspective of the earth were beautiful, but it wasn't the same direct nature connection. It was more like window shopping, or watching it on TV, a very big TV. Now I would have to carry that direct nature connection, that well, inside of me, and also try to get outside into the natural world whenever possible.

As I looked over all the heads sitting quietly in rows I real-ized there were more people on this plane than I had seen in three weeks on the river. I wondered who they were, how they were doing, what they might have been doing for the last three weeks. I reminded myself that every one of them surely had their own stories to tell, just as important to them as mine are to me. Each person, in their way, had their own adventures, their ups and downs, busy and quiet times, on their own real or metaphorical rivers. And each person, like me, probably had things they would change, and things they would not.

The rest of the day involved airports, flying, sitting around, flying some more, and trying to snooze. Running rapids is definitely more fun. I only dozed for about an hour in total. I talked with Jill again twice on airport payphones, and also mailed her a belated anniversary card from the Edmonton airport at midnight.

It was so strange to see the cloak of deep darkness close in on the world through the airport windows in Edmonton, the first truly dark night sky we had seen in three weeks.

Even better: on the leg to Toronto there were stars!

———————

22

I can still hear the water, any time I want. And this is good.

———————

Tuesday, July 30
Day 22
Last day of our trip
Arrival home day
8:00 a.m. Toronto time

We are just taxiing out for the final short hop. I watched the sun rising as we flew in to Toronto. I can hardly wait to hug Jill and the kids.

There've been many group discussions so far, such as we had after the wreck at Eagle Rock and at various other key times on our trip; around the fire at the confluence of the Mackenzie; in the hotel restaurant back in Norman Wells. I'm sure there will be many more post-trip talks. But right now as this particular journey ends, it is my personal thoughts and hundreds of great memories which are flooding my heart.

Gifts from the Waters   187

After we've all gotten ourselves cleaned up, rested, and back to our routines in the south, there are many gems that will continue to glow inside. The good times, the difficult times, the inner growth, and personal memories, will last each of us a lot longer than any talks about what we should have done, could have done, might have done, and will do if there ever is a next time. But of course we'll have those talks anyway, just like all trippers do, as we remember our comradery, our perseverance, our time in the North.

I watch the sky going by. With my pen I tell myself that I especially want to hang on to: that wild ride in to Willow Handle in the Platypus Porter with Roger, the incredible feelings as the little plane left us and we stood alone in the glorious mountain wilderness, the sound of the water, the water, the water…

I have to cut short my list for now. We've started our descent. The air in and around the plane hisses and rumbles: the whitewater of the sky. I ready myself for landing, for hugs, for home.

———•———

Afterwords

I close my eyes and it's all there: the rush of whitewater, the times together, times alone. My inner music plays, and I'm somewhere out on the water again. You might see me smile.

Far beyond the details of my own adventures, I know that what will stick the very deepest inside of me, years and years from now, will be the well. We were so lucky to have the opportunity to drink deeply from it, to be out there for our time, to experience it fully, to become better people from our journey, and to come home safe.

———•◆•———

The Slide Show

That summer, once we had returned to our loved ones, homes, and busy individual lives, everyone got caught up on the things that had been happening while we were away. As promised, Roger put the moose horn in his yard. I gave my silted, grey Tilly hat to my son Patrick. In a wonderful gesture, Otto gave me his own Grey Owl paddle from the trip. Paddy gave me a new knife for my PFD.

We got our photographs processed quickly. Most were slides, since this was before the age of digital photography. Then on a very special, warm, late summer evening, with perfect weather, the group got back together in the big back yard of our Weir family home for a post-trip reunion barbecue, and "The Great Mountain River Giant Outdoor Slide Show".

All eight paddlers were there, as well as spouses, partners, kids, and friends. Everything was set up outside, with chairs, blankets and lots to eat. Kevin and Roger borrowed a huge collapsible movie screen. Roger had collected everyone's slides and co-ordinated them using two slide projectors, so that when the show began everyone would see a professional looking dissolve between each pair of images. Nowadays this is pretty easy to do, thanks to modern computers, but it was quite the high-tech show for us in 1991.

When it got dark, we showed everyone the wonderful images on the big screen. It was dazzling. For a time we were all taken so very far away. The crowd loved it! After we'd gone through all our pictures, we did it over again, this time with animated vocal commentaries, and a considerable dose of humour. It was a truly memorable, happy follow-up ending to our trip.

We heard from our river-guide friends that on their next canoe excursion down the Mountain River, only a couple of weeks after our trip, they had, as requested, looked out for our dam at the exact Eagle Rock location. As we had expected, there was no remnant of it whatsoever that they could find. The river had no-traced the place. No doubt every small cairn of stones that I had built for Jill along the way was also soon knocked over with the winds and rain, and had turned back into simple little piles of pebbles.

They also told us that Frank Pope had actually gone ahead and put our Mary Ellen Carter the Second on display out in front of the Norman Wells Museum for a time! That made us very happy. A couple of years later we heard that he then had her in his own front yard, as a flower planter. I'd love to see it someday.

The Videos

WILDERNESS IS LIKE A WELL…

FOR OUR SOULS.

WE DRINK FROM IT WHEN WE CAN
AND EVEN WHEN WE CAN'T
THE WELL IS STILL THERE
FOR OUR SPIRITS TO FLY TO
…AT ANY TIME.

Over a loud audio track of roaring whitewater, these words scroll slowly up the black movie screen in the opening frames of one of our post-trip videos, and again at its closing.

I'm happy to say that this video, called *Mountain Memories*, and another of our videos called *Spirit of Eagle Rock*, each lasting eight minutes, were shown in the spring of 1992 at the Waterwalker Film and Video Festival in Ottawa, and given Honourable Mention. They were co-created by Otto Schreiber, Roger Michon and I, with help from some others, using video and photographs taken by the eight of us on our trip. We worked on these two films for months in the fall and winter after returning from the Mountain River. With permission, we included parts of the songs "The Mary Ellen Carter" by Stan Rogers, "Colleen's Song" ("Some day...") by Michael Peter Smith, and also my friend Norm Hacking's song, "This One's the Dreamer."

Although we surely experienced some very tough times on our trip, it was an absolutely wonderful journey. We were happy to have the opportunity to share some of it on video with others.

Everyone especially liked the part where we pulled the boat free.

———•—•———

The present written record has taken me a lot longer to finish: twenty-two years. This, in spite of the fact that I have intended to write it ever since I first got home in late July of 1991. But life is busy, and I can be quite a procrastinator. Or maybe this has simply been the best time to share this story again, and more fully; finally the right time to dig out my old Mountain River trip journal, photographs, notes, maps, videos and sketches, to talk again with my paddling friends, to think deeply about everything, and finish writing this one down.

I'm now retired from paid teaching, and am doing other things. Jill and I continue to get out into the wild as often as we can, and we love it. Whenever I get the chance I still enjoy sitting around a smoky campfire listening to the stories of other travellers.

Our three great kids are currently twenty-two years older than they were when their dad paddled the Mountain River. Now grown and moved away from our family home to their own homes, they still love the natural world. All of them are having marvellous adventures, as they travel their own journeys.

My personal metaphorical river also continues along. I've had quite a few other trips under my paddle since the Mountain River days, and hope to continue to canoe for as long as I'm able. Even when someday I can no longer sit in a boat, there will be memories of countless times on the waters, and the many gifts that the waters have given me. I am filled with gratitude.

Phil Weir
Ottawa, 2013

From left to right: Brian Conway, Bert Waslander, Pat O'Shea, Odile Waslander, Phil Weir, Roger Michon, Kevin Conway, Otto Schreiber

Photo by unknown photographer from rafter-kayaker group.

Acknowledgements

Thanks to the river.

Special thanks go to all of my fellow Mountain River paddlers: Roger Michon, Otto Schreiber, Kevin Conway, Odile Waslander, Bert Waslander, Brian Conway and Pat O'Shea. There would have been no trip without them. They were called upon several times to help clarify my memory, and each also gave welcome suggestions. While this story is written from my personal point of view, I tried to keep aware that every one of the others also has their own trip stories, seen from their perspective. Hundreds of trip photographs, taken by the eight of us, helped me with some of the details. Our two eight-minute post-trip videos, *Mountain Memories* and *Spirit of Eagle Rock,* were also valuable resources.

Kevin Conway was especially encouraging and helpful to me, sharing his professional knowledge, and Joan Conway too was insightful and thorough in her recommendations. Marty Hamer maintained steady faith in the project, and very kindly gave extensive time, support, and editing suggestions. Ron Williamson also gave many ideas and long-term encouragement. I was very fortunate to receive several insightful suggestions from Ken Buck. Roy MacSkimming, James Raffan and Romola Thumbadoo also helpfully shared their knowledge.

Chi Meegwetch to elders and other friends who carry and share First Nations teachings.

I also wish to express my deep appreciation for the inspiring books and films of the late great Bill Mason, where he shared his passion and knowledge about canoeing and the wild.

Each of our children, Jody, Daniel and Patrick, strongly supported this project in important ways, and generously shared their ideas and skills.

Most of all I want to thank Jill, my wonderful, ever-encouraging, patient, and tremendously supportive best friend and wife. She has helped me in millions of ways.

Lastly, my thanks to all the paddlers, campers and other friends I've known and learned from over the years – especially those who might have heard me tell part of this story somewhere, sometime, and encouraged me to write it down.

———•·•———

About the Author

Phil Weir was born in downtown Toronto in 1951. Thanks to his family, groups like the Boy Scouts, and summer camps, he escaped the city on treasured trips into the wild, and developed an enduring love of nature and canoeing. He graduated from the University of Toronto  in 1972, where he met and married Jill McNamee. In 1973 Phil and Jill moved to Ottawa and both eventually became teachers. They had three children, and the family did hundreds of wonderful camping trips together. As a high school teacher Phil always found ways to include Outdoor Education. This was done via field trips, clubs, leading and promoting an Outdoor Ed. credit course, curriculum development and also full-time teaching outdoors for five years at the MacSkimming Outdoor Education Centre. Now retired from paid teaching, Phil still enjoys encouraging people to know, to understand, and to love the natural world, and their place in it.

Lightning Source UK Ltd.
Milton Keynes UK
UKHW011802311019
352615UK00001B/86/P